Teachable Moments

Short Stories to
Spark Diversity Dialogue

Teachable Moments
Short Stories to
Spark Diversity Dialogue

By

STEVE L. ROBBINS, PH.D.

PageFree Publishing, Inc.

Advance Praise for Teachable Moments

"I met Steve when he came to our organization to help us link diversity and in clusion to creativity and innovation. His insight, knowledge and stories taught us the importance of becoming intentional about inviting different perspective to the table and being willing to include them. "Teachable Moments" are about that they open a new door to a 21st century dialogue about mindfulness, respect and caring in the business environment."

> Magda Nowak, Director, Organization Capability, PepsiCo International

"Steve has a gift for capturing personal experiences and drawing his audience into talking about powerful issues. As a trainer he has enabled us to begin cru cial conversations needed to effect culture change"

> Sharon M. Wong, Special Assistant for Diversity, NASA/Goddard Space Flight Center

"A powerful storyteller and communicator, Steve has a one of a kind ability to bring difficult, often complex diversity issues to a space where everyone can be involved in the conversation. Insightful, humorous and challenging, these stories are a great way to engage anyone and any organization into sustained diversity dialogue."

> Michael F. Ramirez, Director Inclusiveness & Corporate Diversity, Her man Miller, Inc.

"Steve is a master communicator and a wonderful storyteller who not only keeps your interest, but also gives profound insight into the world we live in today. If you're trying to start a diversity dialogue in your organization, get "Teachable Moments." It's a quick, humorous read, has many valuable insights, and will surely engage people into what Steve calls crucial conversations."

> Wayne Boatwright, Corporate Vice President of Cultural Diversity, Me ridian Health

"Dr. Steve Robbins has a gift and I'm so glad he is sharing it with everyone through this book! Teachable Moments provides moments everyone can relate to and learn from this is a great read!"
    Concetta Itchon, Sr. Diversity Specialist, Campbell Ewald Advertising

With an amazing and powerful life story as his foundation, Steve has captured the essence of why we should all engage in the work of diversity and inclusion it's because all people matter! Like no other person, Steve brings the mes sage of inclusion to life in an inspirational way. Read Teachable Moments and be touched by his gentle, yet persuasive challenge to overcome "unintentional intolerance" for all of us to be better citizens."
    Joseph R. Swedish, President and CEO, Trinity Health

"Whether bringing an audience of hundreds of people to their feet during a Key note address, or sharing his insights through the words of his first book, Steve L. Robbins, Ph.D. is a definite path-maker. His use of humor and real life examples are catalysts for opening the minds of many and providing them with the tools to better understand (and appreciate) the importance of diversity and inclusion – both personally and professionally."
    Michelle Dolieslager, Program Manager – Conferences, SHRM.

"Dr. Robbins has a unique ability to bring fresh and insightful perspectives to the issue of diversity. His inviting, humorous and yet challenging approach brings everyone to a 21st century diversity discussion and allows them recognize their role in developing an inclusive work environment."
-   Glenn M. Winfree, Senior Diversity Consultant, Office of Diversity, Aetna

"Dr. Robbins is a gifted speaker and story teller who can move people to see things they may never have seen before. His knowledge of diversity issues is only surpassed by his ability to share that knowledge in an inviting, insightful and inspirational way. Read Teachable Moments and you'll see what I mean."
    Lynsey Martin, Human Resources LDP, Raytheon

"Everyone and every organization desiring to be more culturally competent needs to engage in meaningful dialogue, and I can't think of a better way to do that than to read Teachable Moments. Dr. Robbins is a truly gifted story teller and teacher who can do what few people can communicate his vast knowledge of diversity in a manner that brings everyone into the conversation."
    Gina M. Bono, Director, HR Planning and Project Management
Organization Development & Talent Management, Trinity Health System

When I first heard Dr. Robbins I was blown away. He is not only an extremely engaging speaker, but his knowledge and passion about his subject matter are *apparent. RARELY have I heard someone on this type of subject matter, where I got much out of it, or felt the speaker had much to teach me. Dr. Robbins is the exception. He is fabulous! Everyone who hears him will walk away a better human being.*

Martha Torre Carter, V.P., Broadcast Production Manager, Campbell Ewald Advertising

"Some people have great knowledge, but can't communicate. Others can com municate but fall short on knowledge. Dr. Robbins comes with the ultimate pack age. He is both very knowledgeable and a great communicator who not only knows his stuff, but also knows how to touch people and move them to take action. If you've heard him speak you know what I mean. If you haven't, read Teachable Moments and take a peek at his fresh perspectives on life and diver sity."

Rita Hubbard Robinson, JD, Executive Director, City of Buffalo Com mission on Citizens' Rights and Community Relations

ISBN 1 58961 512 3 Paperback
ISBN 1 58961 533 6 Hardcover

Published by PageFree Publishing, Inc.
P.O. Box 60
Otsego, Michigan 49078
www.pagefreepublishing.com

Table of Contents

Justice requires those who suffer the least to speak up the most."
~ Steve L. Robbins ~

Preface

LET me say this right off the bat, I am not by profession a writer. However, like everyone else I have a story to tell. In fact I have 33 of them contained in this, my first book. Stories make an effective vehicle for teaching and learning, and are powerful lenses into the human experience. Stories can expose our deep est torments and uncover our greatest triumphs. They can inspire and motivate. They can cause laughter and tears. They have the ability to challenge and inflict great discomfort. All this and more is the potential of storytelling. I do not prom ise to reach all these literary possibilities with the stories in this book, but I have tried to provide a glimpse.

And so I embark on an attempt to tell you some stories—so we can together learn and, at least temporarily, be moved to another reality. The stories in these pages come from various places drawn out of my own experiences. Most are my best recollection of my encounters with life and living, attached with what writ ers call "literary flair." Some stories have my own family members among the cast of characters. Various details in these stories may be disputed by my family members at some point, but heck, that's what wound up in my memory (as faulty as it is). My kids can mischaracterize me when they write their own book.

Other stories are fictional accounts that ask you to imagine a slightly new world using different input data. Hopefully some are able to put you in the moc casins of others so that you may learn from both the joy and pain of others' journeys. All are intended to "spark diversity dialogue."

Such dialogue is the initial step in having what I call "crucial conversa tions"—conversations we shy away from because they may create some cog nitive dissonance, as if a little dissonance every now and then is a bad thing. Yet these are the very conversations that are required to overcome an apparent inability to reconcile unity with diversity, uniqueness with uniformity, certainty with curiosity.

We tend not to have crucial conversations around issues of diversity and in clusion because we often lack the ability. We don't practice it much, and thus aren't very good at it. What is saddening is that we are growing up generations of young people who will also lack the capability of crucial conversations be cause we don't teach them to do it, or how to do it. Yes, we have young people who are more open to "diversity" than past generations, but there's a catch.

As I have noticed young peoples' willingness to enter diversity dialogue is dependent on whether the dialogue will be celebratory in nature, will it be what I call "tamale talk." By this I mean that the way we go about teaching kids about diversity and multi cuturalism has often been centered around celebrating dif ferences. Does the following ring familiar, "Let's have a luncheon on Friday to celebrate diversity. We'll have Jose bring in some tamales. We'll ask Long to wear some Vietnamese clothes, and Tawanna will teach us an African dance."

Don't get me wrong, celebrating diversity is a wonderful thing to do, but if kids learn that diversity is always celebratory, then they will expect fun celebra tions when the topic of diversity pops up. And when diversity dialogue is not fun as it sometimes is not, (Ask here: How does one effectively address issues of racism, sexism and other forms of oppression without getting uncomfortable?) young folks will walk away, either mentally or physically or both, when the talk becomes a little tough. We as a society have not given our young people the words, the willingness and the where with all to have crucial conversations around diversity related issues. We don't give them practice time with tough issues and so many are unable to perform when pushed onto the stage of real ity—of real racism, real sexism, real homophobia, real classism, real ageism, real discrimination, real oppression, real… etc.

We must model what we desire in our young folks. In this case, we must show them how to talk about tough diversity related issues—to have crucial conversa tions. And for us to do it well, we have to practice. The stories contained in this book offer the meat for us to chew if we desire to have a dialogue on diversity. I invite you to use these stories to practice diversity dialogue, to hone your abili ties to talk about the warts in our not so fun and not so celebratory history. A just and united future depends on it.

Many of the stories in these pages were originally written as the "Teach able Moments" section of the "Do Diversity Right" electronic newsletter I once wrote. That newsletter is now called "Inclusion Insights" (you can still get it for free at my Web site, www.SLRobbins.com).

When the stories were first distributed I received many emails and phone calls from readers who said they "really" enjoyed them. Many also asked of they could forward the stories to others or put them in their own publications. I was thrilled and humbled by the affirming response. Eventually someone asked if I was ever going to put the growing collection of stories in a book. I quickly said yes. Not so quick was actually doing it, but here it is.

I've tried to employ humor in a number of stories to get serious and not so serious point across. Research and my own experience suggest that humor helps to break down defenses. As many of you know, the world of "diversity and inclusion" is filled with defensive walls. Some are intentional. Some aren't. Regardless, they still exist and we who may call ourselves "diversity profession als" must deal with them strategically. My strategy at times is humor. It fits my closet desire to be a comedian. My attempts at humor are not to make light of serious issues, but are serious attempts to shed maybe a different light on the hu man experience. Where I fail at humor, please be gentle in your critique. Where I succeed smile a wide smile and share it with others. Either way, try to find the nuggets of insight I call "Teachable Moments."

I hope you will be able to find use for the book in your life and in the organi zations of which you are a part. Use the book to practice having crucial conversa tions. Use it to potentially reframe the work of diversity and inclusion. Use it to glean a perspective you may have never considered. Use it to invite others into a dialogue that will hopefully lead to crucial, yet unconventional conversations. Most of all use it to remind yourself and others that everyone has unique stories, and these unique stories can help give us glimpses into realities (and opportuni ties) we could not imagine on our own. That is the power of story.

The book begins with my own story of why I do this work. Read it before you read the other stories to give you a better context for why everyone should be engaging in the work of diversity and inclusion. Not to give everything away, but in the end it's all about caring about other people and putting others before self. If we all were able to do that, I imagine we might not need many books like this. That would be a good thing, since I have found it difficult to be a pretend writer.

We can strive for unity without requiring uniformity.
~ Steve L. Robbins ~

Acknowledgements

MY mom always taught me that any accomplishment or achievement I might have is because I walk on a path made clear by the many who toiled before me. Many times as I was not displaying humility and selflessness, she would step in to remind me that I could be a path maker or path blocker. I never fully grasped what she was saying as a youngster. I do now. And so I need and want to thank some people for clearing the paths in my life, and to this book

First, I thank my family beginning with my wife Donna who has put up with my undeniable quirkiness, allowing me to pursue a vocational calling that is not always easy on a family of six. Her "steady as she goes" personality and un conditional love and support create the anchor for me, and our family when we have encountered the unpredictable winds of life. I try often not to quote from Tom Cruise movies, but in this case his words are fitting, "Donna, You complete me!"

I am grateful to my kids, Nicholas, Zachary, Jacob and Natalie for allowing me to be their fallible father (and for the inspiration for many of the humorous parts of this book). My kids are great, and I don't tell them that enough so here it is in print—Nicholas, Zachary, Jacob and Natalie you are great and I love you very much! Forgive me when I falter.

A special thanks goes to my "adopted family," mom and dad Wyn, brothers Tod, Matt, Mark and Joe who helped to fill a big hole in my life following my mother's death. Much gratitude goes to brother Tod (who is the doctor in the family you go to if you have some type of physical ailment) for not cutting me from his college music group. It's simply amazing how a chance encounter of two apparently very different people in a musical audition can grow into the unbreakable bonds of family.

I would also be remiss if I did not acknowledge the family I gained when I married Donna, the Lennemans. Thanks mom and dad Lenneman, Gary, Ann, Mary, Rita for unconditionally accepting a Vietnamese kid from the city into your German family on the farm, and for leaping beyond stereotypes to see how a 5'7" Vietnamese guy could be a life match for your 6' blonde, German hottie! Also, without all of you I would not know the invigorating signature smells of farm life.

An unfathomable amount of thanks goes to my mother, Nguyen Dung (Nancy), who literally sacrificed her life so that I might have the opportunity of life, liberty and the pursuit of happiness. The lessons you taught me about family, perseverance, sacrifice, humility and balance continue to shape me today, even in your physical absence. I hope your little Long is making you proud.

Most of all, thank you to my Lord and Savior Jesus Christ who gives me life, hope and purpose, who is my foundation. I have a thankful heart for what you have done and continue to do for me. Thank you for putting together the broken pieces of my life and creating a servant with eternal purpose. Please tell my mom and sister Diane I miss them and love them very much.

Others who have played a significant part in the Steve Long-Nguyen Robbins building project include my many friends in Kennewick, Washington, especially Dennis, Todd, Craig, Paul and Marty; Dr. Quentin Schultze, who gave me a "B" on my first paper (I was not used to B's) at Calvin College and beneath the grade wrote, "Whom much is given, much is required"; the scholars and teachers in the Communication Department at Michigan State University especially Dr. Charles Atkin and Dr. William Donohue, who honed my critical thinking skills and made graduate school challenging and fun; Dr. Harry Knopke and Mr. Bob Woodrick for giving me the opportunity to be the first director of the Woodrick Institute for the Study of Racism and Diversity at Aquinas College. I have missed many others who played a part in who I have become. Thank you all for your friendships, support and encouragement. You've all made a tremendous difference in my life, and have helped to put me on the path I am walking (sometimes running) on today.

To put the world in order, we must first put the nation in order; to put the nation in order, we must put the family in order; to put the family in order, we must cultivate our personal life; and to cultivate our personal life, we must first set our hearts right.

~ Confucius ~

Introduction

AS I travel across the global landscape working with various organizations and businesses I am often asked if I get tired doing this work—of this thing some have called "diversity and inclusion." My response is a balanced one, "yes and no," I say. The travel and being away from my family is always difficult. Some people I run across, for various reasons, just don't seem to want or be able to embrace the reality of a more diverse world. They can't seem to give up old 20th century scripts that don't work so well in a 21st century world. These types of folks can at times make the work tiresome. They also make it enlightening and invigorating.

So, on the one hand, yes, I do get tired. On the other hand I do not. I am energized and sustained by a life calling that became clear to me in a crucible of cruelty. It is from that crucible that I get my sustenance and passion for this work. So let me tell you that story.

I immigrated to the United States in 1970. In the midst of an escalating war in Vietnam my mother married an American serviceman, not because she loved him, but so she could bring me to the United States. Let me give you a little context for how difficult that decision was for my mom.

In Vietnamese culture family is revered and valued. Family defines who you are, why you exist. We don't just say we value family. We actually do it! The elderly aren't sent away. They are taken in. We don't get upset if a relative drops in unannounced. We break out the Pho (beef noodle soup)! Family bonds are strong.

And so my mom made the excruciating decision to leave her family behind to ensure her young son would have life. Note here that I did not say, "have a life."

The danger of death was an everyday reality. She left her mother and father, five brothers and sisters, a bunch of aunts and uncles and cousins. Family in Vietnam is not just mom, dad and the kids the way we in the U.S. tend to think of it. She packed very little (because we had very little) and, with her five year old son in hand, literally traveled half way around the world to another world.

When we arrived in Los Angeles I am sure my mom was thinking she had made a mistake. As you might imagine being Vietnamese in the U.S. in the 1970s was not a great time to be Vietnamese. I imagine how she felt is how many Middle Eastern folks and Mexican (and other Latino/Hispanic) immigrants (legal and illegal) feel today. Standing no more than 4 feet, 11 inches tall and speaking with a heavy accent, my mom was a convenient target for unwarranted discrimi nation. These injustices invaded her life with regularity, and there was little she could do.

The Los Angeles area neighborhoods we lived in were not so nice to me either. Many times I would come home covered in blood from fights I found myself in. Some fights I started. Others I did not. Many were because I was the different kid from the war with slanty eyes. As the saying goes, "kids can be cruel."

Following these brawls I would find my way to our apartment home where my mom would pull me into her arms and hold me tight for minutes on end. She rarely said anything as she wiped the blood from me with a warm cloth. She didn't have to – the tears streaming down her face said it all. She was in much pain. I really didn't understand what my mom was going through on these occa sions. I think I do now.

My mom thought she had brought us to a better place. Undeniably the U.S. was a much better place to be in at the time, but it wasn't the place she was told about. It wasn't the concept she held in her head. It wasn't, "we hold these truths to be self evident… that among those rights are life, liberty and the pursuit of happiness." It didn't live out those famous words penned by Thomas Jefferson.

Little by little the injustices chipped life away from my mom. The man she married turned out not to be the coolest guy. He forced my mom to have an abor tion (my mom was raised with Catholic influences). I still remember the day we went to the hospital for the procedure. I didn't know what was happening at the time. I just recall my mom and I going to the hospital, she in a visibly distraught emotional place. When we left, she once again had tears running down her gentle face. When I later found out as a teenager why we had gone to the hospital I was filled with an unforgettable pain, and anger.

For many reasons I was never close to my stepfather, that un cool guy. But he found his way to be close to my sister Diane, his flesh and blood daughter. He was convicted of sexually assaulting my sister in 1984. To this day I still do not know when these awful offenses began, I just know they ended up with my sister running away from home with a friend in the summer of 1986 when she was 14 years old. It was later that summer that my mom received a phone call that would devastate her life.

The man on the other end of the call, a King County Sheriff's detective, delivered the horrible message that the girl my sister had run away with was found, murdered in the Seattle area. When my mom asked about my sister, the detective could only offer a glimmer of hope, "we have been unable to locate your daughter Mrs. Robbins." I remember my mom falling to her knees, sobbing so hard her body shook violently. My mom was a woman of few words. No words were necessary to know how my mom felt at this moment. Though there was the chance my sister was still alive, most likely in grave conditions, I think my mom knew her family was now short one life. I knew it too.

I headed back to college in Michigan that Fall with a heavy heart weighted down by the knowledge that I likely would never see my sister again and the pain of knowing my mom was suffering so greatly. In her small frame was the strongest woman I had ever known, will ever know. But no amount of strength could lift the enormity of the hurt that crushed my mom's spirit every hour of every day. She did her best to mask that pain from me every time we talked on the phone, but sometimes there was no hiding it. No one knew it at the time, but in the solitude of my dorm room that year heavy tears often flowed from me eyes.

My mom tried to take her own life in 1989. I had no knowledge of this until very recently when a friend of mine from Washington showed me a videotape of my mom appearing on a Seattle area television program. It was a program about parents who had lost their child. On the videotape was a dispirited woman visibly distressed from the cumulative events of her life. The woman on the screen was my mom but she was not. Asked about how she copes day to day, she told the program host she continues the struggle for one reason, her son.

The next two years I'm sure we difficult for my mom, but she never let on, always protecting me from the pain that wreaked havoc on her emotional, spiritual and physical being.

June 1991 was a wonderful, happy time etched into my life, and I suspect my mom's. That's when I married my wife Donna, a stunningly beautiful woman inside and out who filled gaps in my life, many unknown by me at the time.

My mom and Donna hit it off right away, though from casual observation they looked to be very different. A mental picture of their first meeting sticks with me today. My mom is embracing my future wife with a hug often reserved for long standing family members and friends. It's kind of an odd scene, this 4' 11" dark-haired Vietnamese woman locked together with a nearly 6' blonde, German that would one day be her daughter. It would take nearly fifteen years before I recognized how that first meeting would come to symbolize the work that I do.

Five months following my wedding, I was thick into my graduate studies at Michigan State University when I received a phone call from my mom who was back home in Washington State. We shared with each other the events of our lives that past week, though I do not recall the specifics. Before ending our conversation, my mom softly said, "Long, you have Donna to take care of you now. I love you very much." I told my mom I loved her too, and looked forward to our next phone call. The next phone call from Washington State was not from my mom.

A little more than a week after talking with my mom the phone rang in the duplex Donna and I called our first home. Donna answered, and following a brief conversation handed the phone to me. Sitting on the bed in our bedroom, I found myself speaking with an officer from the Benton County Sheriffs Department. He asked if I was Steve Robbins, and if I knew a woman named Nancy Robbins. "Yes," I said, "That's my mother." Thoughts, many unsettling, were running in my head at this moment as a short silence fell onto the conversation.

"Mr. Robbins, I am sorry to have to tell you, but we just found your mother."

"Is she okay?" I asked.

"I'm sorry sir, but your mother was found in her bathroom and she was not alive." Shaking, I asked what happened. "Apparently your mother took her own life. She had hanged herself from the showerhead."

I could not say anything as the weight of the pain crushed my vocal chords, and my spirit. I just shook as the tears welled up and a lifetime of events, good and bad, raced through my mind. I really don't recall much after that. I do remember the waves of pain that rocked my body.

A few days later I was in my mother's apartment in Washington State sifting through her belongings, trying to comprehend what had happened, what was happening. Many questions drummed through my head. Why did my mom choose this path? Why didn't I see the signs? Why wasn't I there for her? The answers were nowhere to be found. The questions only ignited more questions, and my quest to answer them tormented my sleepless nights.

The more I thought about what my life would be like without my mom, the more I began to reflect upon what my life had been like. Many things that I had somehow sunk to the deepest depths of my mind surfaced. Not all were pretty. I came face to face with the reality that I did not like myself much. More specifically, I did not like being Asian, being Vietnamese, being me.

More questions busied my thoughts. How does someone who looks like me get the name Steve Robbins? Why do I have a perm? Why have I had a perm since Junior High? How come I can find Asian women attractive, but have never been inclined to date one? In a different context, these questions might be a bit funny. In this particular context, they burdened my soul. Recognizing that you've spent a lifetime suppressing large parts of your true self is extremely disconcerting.

After burying my mom, I returned to Michigan with more questions than answers. A chapter in my life had been closed, and new ones were to begin. At the time I did not know what would be written on those future pages, I just knew I had to press on.

As I look back today, I see how the painful experience of my mom's death shaped who I am and what I do now. It was her death that led me to become more interested and sensitive to issues of diversity. It led me to a deeper self examination—one that would tear scabs off old wounds, but would also lead me to the core of who I am, of who my mom taught me to be. I would come to understand and put a label on the hate I had for myself. In the world of race studies, it is called "internalized racism." I hated myself because the messages I encountered in the world taught me to hate me. I had internalized the many nega tive messages about Asians, and specifically Vietnamese people.

The many people who discriminated against my mom and me I remembered to be white. That, however, did not teach me to hate white people, it taught me to want to be white because white people were not being discriminated against. As I was able to more fully understand what was happening, the more I was able to come to appreciate who I really I am, and what my mom had been trying to teach me all along about my heritage and history.

To be honest, I am still dealing with internalized racism today. I suspect I will be dealing with it the rest of my life. But that's okay, I better understand the "dis-ease" within me and how it plays out in society. I also understand what I've been called to do. All my past experiences, the good and bad, the beautiful and ugly, have equipped me to do the work that I do around diversity, and I do this work to honor my mom.

My mom literally sacrificed 26 years of her life to make sure that I could have a life. She faced cruelty many times, too many times, during her short 47 years on this planet. I am certain she was not the only one. Many others face a similar pain today. The reality of people needlessly suffering motivates me to do the work that I do.

When I go out to speak and work with organizations, I am going out a bit selfishly. You see, I want people to understand that the work around diversity, inclusion and cultural competency is not about political correctness or about a better bottom line. Neither is about protecting against a lawsuit or compliance. It's not even about changing demographics. No, at its core this work is about car ing about other people, treating them with dignity and respect because they are human beings who deserve such. It's about standing up for justice in the face of injustice.

I believe the negative "baggage" around "diversity" was created and is car ried forth by people who are blind, at least partially, to the myriad realities of our world, and who have not fully realized that doing the work of "diversity" is truly about being a nice, caring and compassionate citizen. It's my guess that the vast majority people would like to be called nice, caring and compassionate. A large part of my work is to urge, encourage and teach others to walk the talk of "nice, caring and compassionate." If more of us would sincerely and genuinely do that,

19

our world would be a much better place—a place where fairness and justice would rule.

I do this work to honor my mom and to do my part in making sure that fewer people face what my mom faced. Why? Because I imagine that if, while my mom was alive, more people would have stood up for justice, as a shield between her and injustice; if more people would have protected her from the cruelty of ignorant and un mindful people; if more people would have said, "You can't do that to her because she is a human being who deserves better treatment"; if more people would have done those things in the midst of my mom's tears I know that my four children would have a grandmother to play with today.

So, I do this work because I know firsthand the mountaintops and valleys of our world, and I want more people to experience the mountaintops. I can't and don't want to do this work alone, and so I go out to touch people so that we can walk with one another, side by side in making this a better place, especially for the generations that will come.

Yes, I know this all sounds very idealistic and pie in the sky, but as Dr. Mar tin Luther King Jr. so eloquently said, "I've seen the mountaintop" and it's a wonderful place. Let's all work together to be path makers, creating many paths to the mountaintop. It will be hard, painful work, an uphill battle littered with unbearable mindsets and seemingly insurmountable circumstances. Yes, it will be that and likely more. There will be times when you will want to give up. I have experienced those times on many occasions. In those times do what I do; I imagine my mom sitting on the floor telling my four kids the wisdom-filled stories she told me as a kid, and as she finishes she gives them all a great big hug. Before they all get up to leave, my mom tells my children to love and take care of each other, and to be path makers, not path blockers.

There is a Chinese proverb that says, "Tall trees face strong winds." I invite you to be a tall tree with me. Read the stories in this book with the context I have given you. Share the stories with others to spark diversity dialogue. Practice cru cial conversations. Take advantage of teachable moments. Do all this and more to become a "tall tree," and when the strong winds hit know that there are other tall trees in your presence working among you, with you and for you. You are never alone in doing this good work. Good work is never done alone.

Ready?

We don't see things as they are. We see things as we are.
~ Anais Nin ~

1
The Right Environment

THERE is a small pond on our property that provides my family all sorts of fun. In the winter, it's a makeshift skating rink that allows me to prove over and over again that humans were not designed to dwell on ice nor should two sharp blades be attached to shoes as a mode of traveling. Come summer time, after the bruises have faded from my rear, the pond transforms into a delightful fishing hole.

I had been told that when the pond was created a number of years ago, it was stocked with bass and various pan fish. These fish have thrived in the pond with very little human intervention. Despite cold Michigan winters and warm, muggy summers they flourish. The environment suits them rather well.

If you enjoy fishing and have kids, as I do, there is nothing much better than having a pond stocked with fish right in your front yard. And if these fish are bass and pan fish, that's just icing on the cake. Why, you ask? Let's just say in telligence is not among their strengths, especially the pan fish. Or, as my 4-year old Zachary says, "Dad, these fish aren't very smart are they?" Put another way, if these species were the only kind people fished for, there would be no need for fish stories. The only thing difficult about catching these fish is making sure they don't swallow your hook.

I get a kick out of fishing with my kids in our pond. On these occasions I rarely get to drop my own line in the water, partly because I spend a good deal of time untangling my kids' lines, putting worms on hooks and making sure fish

21

are the only creatures being hooked. If you ever want a random body piercing, I invite you to join us for an afternoon of fishing. I also do not fish much in our pond because bobber fishing with a worm for bass and pan fish holds little ap peal for me. Yes, you might me call one of those nose-in-the-air, snobby fisher people known as fly-fishers. But I'm really not. Bobber fishing with a worm is not beneath me at all, especially when I'm being skunked with my fly rod by a little creature with the brain the size of a small pea. Catching fish is always better than not catching fish. But with that said, I like challenges, and, to me, fly-fishing is a more inviting challenge.

I don't fly-fish for just any 'ole species. Some of my younger years were spent in the Pacific Northwest, where the fish of choice is trout. For me, it was Rain bow trout. I fondly remember warm summer days when my mom would take me to a creek near our home and let me fish the day away. I spent hours "hunting" Rainbows up and down the creek. Although they were planted fish, they were not easy to catch, especially for a 10-year-old. They are smart, wary fish that chal lenge the fisherperson to think about how to approach them, how to present the bait.

While Rainbows can be difficult to catch, when you get one on, well, that's an appropriate reward for a plan well executed. Hooking into a big Rainbow was one of the more exciting things I had done up to that point in my life. Watch ing a Rainbow jump out of the water flashing its namesake range of colors is a beautiful sight. Suffice it to say, I have an affinity for Rainbow trout, something I wanted to pass down to my kids.

That's why I undertook efforts to plant some Rainbows in our pond. I wanted my kids to have the experience of delicately placing a fly in front of a feeding trout, and then waiting for the water's surface to break as the fish sucked in the bait. The fight afterward is great, but it's the presentation and anticipation of a "hit" that makes fly-fishing a great sport. As you might guess, to plant Rainbows you first must have some. So, I searched for a trout farm where I could get some of these beautiful fish. It wasn't easy. There are only a couple farms in Michigan that raise Rainbow trout, and they apparently don't buy into all this stuff called advertising and marketing. After a thorough and nearly futile search, I finally found a trout farm. Excited at the prospect of being able to fly-fish for Rainbows, I called the place.

"Stoney Creek, can I help you?" An enthusiastic young voice answered. I asked her if I could speak with someone about obtaining some Rainbow trout. "I'll get my dad," she said.

After a few minutes I heard a voice from the other end of the line, "Yes, this is Steve. I hear you need some information about our trout."

I told Steve that I wanted to plant some Rainbows in our pond and he quickly asked me a number of questions regarding the size of the pond, its water source, what types of fish are in it now, etc. I answered as best I could, "...half-acre... underground spring...bass and pan fish."

"Hmmm," Steve responded. "Do you know the temperature of the water?"

"It gets into the 70's during the summer," I answered.

Again Steve responded with a, "Hmmm." Some type of language he picked up from being around fish all day, I surmised. "I don't think the environmental conditions as you've described them are well-suited for Rainbows."

"Why's that?" I asked, surprised that there wasn't an "Hmmm" in his last remark.

"Rainbows need highly oxygenated, cool water, ideally between 55 and 65 degrees. They can survive at slightly warmer temperatures, but it puts a lot of stress on them."

"So you don't think I can put Rainbows in our pond?" I asked with disappointment in my voice.

"If you do a few things to get more oxygen in the water and put some big logs into the pond to give the trout some shade, they have a good chance of surviving. All you can do is try." He added that making those changes also would benefit the bass and pan fish that already were in the pond - a point I didn't seriously consider at the time.

With renewed excitement I asked if he had the equipment I needed to oxygenate the pond, and he said he had aerators that would do the trick. The logs would be a cinch; we have a number of fallen trees on our property that would be perfect for the job. I then asked him how many trout I should get and what size they should be. Steve asked me how big the bass were in the pond. "The largest one I've caught is 18 inches," I said.

"Hmmm," the fish talk was back in Steve's vocabulary.

With cautious optimism I queried, "What's the problem?"

"No problem," he said. "Just that you'll have to get some big trout. Bass can eat fish nearly as big as them, or at least they'll try. If you don't get the right size trout, they won't have much of a chance in a small pond like yours. You'll need 10- to 12-inch trout to be safe. About 25 to 30 of them will do." Our interesting and enlightening conversation ended with Steve giving me directions to his trout farm.

A few days later I drove out to Steve's farm and picked up the trout and the aerator I needed. He reiterated the need to set up the aerator quickly and to get the logs in the water, not only for shade but to provide some cover and safety for the trout. He was concerned that relocating the trout would make them weak and vulnerable to the bass, so they needed places to hide. I told him I would get everything set up pronto.

I brought the trout home, and with kid like eagerness placed them in the water. They all survived the trip, and after getting their bearings, they swam off into the deeper parts of the pond. I then began to set up the aerator, but it was getting dark and a refreshing Michigan evening rain had begun. I told myself I would get to the aerator and the logs the next day.

Well, things at work and around the house got busy. The "next day" turned into "next week" turned into "next month." And as time passed, I noticed some subtle signs that something was wrong. You see, when I first put the Rainbows in, I often watched for rings of water gently disturbing the pond's serene surface, signaling the fish were rising to the top to feed. I knew these were the trout since bass and sunfish rarely do this. Initially, I observed frequent flurries of surface-breaking activity in the morning and evening hours as the trout rose to grab their bug-filled breakfasts and dinners. But over time, the telltale rings disappeared. Once numerous, the observable indicators of trout life gradually faded. By the time I put the aerator and logs into the pond, it was too late.

In their own way, the newly planted trout had been telling me they were strug gling in their new environment. But I didn't listen or pay attention. I assumed that, since they are considered to be strong fish, they would survive until I had the time to create the environment that gave them the best chance for survival. I'm guessing that they either suffocated from lack of oxygen or were too physi cally stressed by the warm water to fend off the bass, or both. I had waited too long, and the trout paid the price.

I learned a valuable lesson about having the right environment when planting trout. No matter how strong and healthy the fish were when I put them in the pond, unless I was willing to change the environment, taking their needs into consideration, I was doomed to lose them. The lesson was an expensive one. Big Rainbow trout aren't cheap.

People are much the same as Rainbow trout when it comes to environments. We place a lot of stress on people when we don't develop environments in which they can survive and, ultimately, thrive. The emotional, cognitive and physical energy it takes to cope with unfriendly and intolerant environments will drain even the best and brightest of their vast potential. The stress eventually takes its toll in the form of inefficiency, poor performance, absenteeism and even poor health. And unlike my situation with the trout, where I take responsibility for the outcome, many organizations "blame" people for their inability to thrive in an environment that's not even conducive to "surviving."

Organizations often blame people for problems that sometimes have their roots firmly but subtly embedded in structures, systems and scripts. What some times are situational, organizational factors depriving "new fish" of a healthy workplace environment are commonly seen as dispositional, individual traits. That is, problems are seen to lie with the individual , and when individuals are seen as the "problem," there is usually little effort taken to uncover systemic is sues of exclusion and intolerance.

Just as there are real and meaningful differences between bass/pan fish and trout and the environments they need, there are real and meaningful differences between "different" people. Whether the differences are between people of color and white folks, or Baby Boomers and Generation Y, or men and women, failure to develop an open minded and respectful organizational environment one that takes the needs of all people into consideration - only makes us less efficient, and hampers our ability to compete with organizations that have created truly inclusive environments for their people.

Like me with the knowledge I gained from trout farmer Steve, some organizations have done their homework and become aware of the meaningful differences that exist among people. They have become enlightened on what it truly means to be diverse and inclusive. But, also like me, some don't do anything with that knowledge. These organizations conceptually understand the need to change their existing environment or culture to prepare for impending demographic changes, but there is no urgency or motivating passion to do so.

Often, there is an underlying belief that the existing environment should be adequate for anyone (because it suits the majority of people already there). But evidence points to the contrary. Indeed, differences do matter. And those organizations that understand this fundamental concept will be the most competitive in the future in terms of recruiting, hiring and retaining "the best and brightest" candidates that demographers say are only growing more diverse.

If I were to do it again, I would put the aerator and logs in the pond well before I put in the trout. The pond would be prepared before the trout arrived, ensuring that I would have given them the best chance for survival. It really doesn't take much on my part to develop the environment in which I know trout, bass and pan fish can survive. If I had done what I knew I needed to do, my family and I would now have the benefit and thrill of catching Rainbows literally right in our front yard. And as trout farmer Steve said to me, when I take the correct steps in making the environment good for the trout, I also make it better for the bass and pan fish. Doing right for some actually can make it better for all. Wow, what a great concept! An inclusive environment that respects the many as well as the few is the hallmark of successful organizations in the 21st century.

What's the state of your environment?

"Discovery consists of seeing what everybody has seen and thinking what nobody has thought."
~ Albert von Szent Gyorgy ~

2
Be Consistent

I once had the opportunity to work with a manufacturing company on its sup plier diversity program. The company was preparing to do more work with the automotive industry and knew it would have little chance getting contracts from the Big Three automakers if it did not have a diverse supplier base.

In meetings with the leadership of the company I learned that it had no rela tionships with minority owned enterprises. Apparently, the company was reluc tant to work with minority owned businesses because of a negative past experi ence.

That experience, the CEO told me, had soured them on even attempting to work with minority owned enterprises. I was intrigued about what had happened and asked about it.

The CEO began, "We had received a big contract from another company, but part of its expectation for us was that we included minority owned businesses as we sought our own suppliers. We had great difficulty finding one, but we did it." He seemed reluctant to go on, expecting me to criticize him and his company for a lack of inclusiveness. I just smiled and asked him to continue.

He went on, "The relationship started out well. We worked together to make sure we would get things out on time with the highest quality. But when the first shipment of parts came from them, it came two days late and there were too many defects. It made us look bad to the company that had given us a big con

tract. But we stuck with the relationship and tried hard
to get it right the second time."

"What happened the second time?" I asked.

"Nothing changed. The second shipment also was late and full o

"Then what did you do?"

The CEO replied, "There was nothing else we could do but break th
lationship and tell our contracting company what happened. Fortunately, we
didn't lose our contract. We found another supplier to do the job, a white owned
firm, and everything worked out." Rather apologetically he added, "We wanted
everything to work out, but it didn't and now we'd rather not deal with minor
ity owned companies. But we know we have to if we want some of the bigger
contracts."

"So that one incident was so bad that you don't want to work with other mi
nority-owned businesses?" I asked.

He replied adamantly, "Yes, I think we have every reason to feel the way we
feel. We almost lost a big contract due to the incompetence of that MBE. You
don't think we did the right thing? You don't think we should feel this way?"

With a calmness that I knew was unexpected I began, "If that minority owned
business knew what was expected from it, said it could do it and didn't deliver
even after being given assistance and a second chance, then you absolutely did
the right thing. You don't want to work with companies that do not perform as
promised." The CEO appeared surprised.

But I continued, "Now answer me this. Have you ever contracted with white
owned companies to provide you services or products and had to break off the
relationship with them because they did not meet expectations?" Without pause
he said, "Of course, that has happened several times."

Then, with a smile, I asked, "And you continue to work with white owned
companies?"

rferes with my learning is my education.
~ Albert Einstein ~

3
A Better Script

RECENTLY, I learned a lesson about how different perspectives and experiences produce different ways of seeing problems and, ultimately, different solutions to those problems. It's an embarrassing story, but I feel compelled to tell you about the power of "cognitive scripts."

The story begins with me being named the CVO of my house, an honor bestowed by my wife, who always is looking to promote to positions of importance. For those of you who may not know, the acronym stands for "Chief Vacuuming Officer." Yes, I am the Chief Vacuuming Officer in my household and I report directly to the CEO, my wife. As you might imagine, as CVO I have the responsibility of vacuuming our house every week…or so. Yes indeed, I am in charge of sucking dust!

As the CVO, I gave myself a nice budget for a vacuum cleaner and quickly spent it on the best cleaner money could buy   at least, that's what the television commercial said. This is no ordinary vacuum cleaner. It has six wheels that all swivel for great maneuverability. Its 6 amp motor has sucking power akin to distant relatives of a newly minted lottery winner. If you want a hose attachment, any hose attachment, this vacuum cleaner has it. I easily could vacuum our drapes…if I ever had the inclination. It has lights to tell you when an area is clean or dirty. And talk about technology, it has this HEPA filter thing that the smallest atom could not get penetrate. (Okay, okay, the filter actually promises that it will trap 99.9998 percent of all harmful particles.) So you get the picture. I bought the best of the best when it comes to vacuum cleaners, a 24th century machine for wreaking havoc on 21st century dust! It is, if I must say so, the mother of all vacuum cleaners!

One day while vacuuming with this technological marvel, I heard a pop and suddenly felt air blowing on my leg. I looked down to see that the door holding the HEPA filter had flung open. "Not a problem," I thought as I reached to close the filter door and resumed my duties. Not long after, however, the filter door flew open again. I turned off the vacuum cleaner to take a closer look, and as I examined the door for problems, I noticed something wrong with the latch. It didn't seem like a big deal, so I tried one more time to see if the door might hold against the pressure of the vacuum. It did not. The latch was broken. And as I said the word "broken," a little script activated in my head and the word "tape" emerged in my thoughts.

At this point I need to let you in on a bit of my past. I am a tape man. That is, if something is broken, I use tape to fix it. Could be any tape - Scotch, electri cal, masking or the mother of all tapes, the Holy Grail of tapes...DUCT TAPE. Where did I learn this? Where did I get this "script?" Well, my stepfather taught me to use tape as a young boy.

When things were broken, his solution was tape. He used tape to fix the torn wings of my paper airplanes, to hem his pants and to seal leaky air hoses in our car. Tape was an easy solution so we always had tape. It wasn't messy, and most of all, tape always seemed to work. When something is broken, tape always comes to mind.

It was no different with my vacuum cleaner. So I retrieved some masking tape out of our desk and placed a strip on the filter door, then turned on the vacuum cleaner. I waited several minutes to see if the door would stay shut. And it did, as I knew it would. "Fixed!"

As I maneuvered the vacuum cleaner through the rooms on our main floor, I pondered the healing qualities of tape. I wondered about the inventor of tape, and why tape was never talked about alongside other great inventions like the wheel, the steam engine, the polio vaccine or the television remote control. Deep into thought and a little distraught about why tape has not received the credit it deserves, I again felt air blowing on my leg. The filter door had swung open again. Quickly I thought, "More tape."

With the roll of masking tape in my hand once again, I strategically placed more strips on the door. After a short while, it resembled a little cocoon. Surely this would hold. I began to vacuum again, but five minutes later the door flew open again. Now, I was getting frustrated. Obviously, I needed more tape. Not more quantity, more quality. Yes, I needed DUCT TAPE!

I walked back to the special place in our house where we keep duct tape. I do not store duct tape alongside mere mortal masking tape. That, of course, would be blasphemy. Duct tape has it's own shrine on a special shelf in our laundry room, far away from the hands of kids who do not understand its mystical heal ing qualities. As I opened the door to get the shiny, silvery gray roll of magic, I could feel my heart rate quickening. It's always thrilling, somewhat spiritual to invoke the power of duct tape. With great care I cut off a small piece and gently made my way back to the vacuum cleaner.

At about this time, my wife emerged from our downstairs dungeon (read: kids area) curious about why the vacuum cleaner was turning on and off so often. She asked what was going on with the duct tape stuck to my hand. As I explained about the filter door, she gave me that look that wives can give their husbands. You know, the one that says, "You're just stupid aren't you?"

Without a word, but with a shake of her head, she walked over to the nearby desk. At first I thought she was reaching for some tape, but her hand emerged holding a little rubber band. "Crazy woman," I thought. But I tried her solution because, after all, she is the CEO. I again began sweeping the carpet, certain that the dainty little rubber band soon would break. Secretly, I wanted the door to fly open, but five minutes went by and then 10. The door remained shut. The rubber band was working. "Please break," I prayed to the tape gods. But the rubber band did not break.

Could it be that rubber bands are superior to tape? I finished vacuuming and the rubber band held. Now my simple tape as a solution to everything broken world was falling apart. From now on, I no longer could just think about tape, I had to think about rubber bands. Flashbacks to the day I realized that Wonder Woman really didn't exist tortured my brain. As my synapses worked to re route themselves, I came to understand that I had just been taught, or actually re taught, a valuable lesson.

So what did I learn? I "learned" what I have been telling others for years. Different people with different experiences often come up with different solutions. In this case, my paradigm for fixing things revolved around tape. But in this instance, tape did not work. I spent at least 30 minutes trying to get tape to work, with no thought of seeking a different solution. On the other hand, my wife fixed the problem in a matter of minutes with her own solution, a rubber band. You see, she is a teacher, and inside a teacher's world are rubber bands. In fact, inside a teacher's world there are many things and experiences that are different than my own. A rubber band was a "natural" option for her. She didn't have to think about it much. Right away, she saw a solution. She did not have to expend a lot of cognitive energy to arrive at a sound solution.

I know that my solution, duct tape, would have worked. Everyone knows that, right? The filter door would have stayed shut with just a small piece of duct tape, but while the solution would have worked, it would not have been as elegant as a rubber band because duct tape always leaves some residue behind once you take it off.

I'm sure tape will always pop into my head as a "first" solution. However, it's likely that I will not have to stretch (pun intended) too far to come up with rub ber bands as a viable alternative. Who knows, I might even go beyond tape and rubber bands.

There's nothing necessarily wrong with having past experiences guide pres ent actions. That's natural. But knowing that past experiences may not neces sarily yield effective solutions to present day problems should make us open to myriad, diverse experiences—experiences that prompt multiple options the next time we face a problem. Along those lines, it's probably a good thing to have people around us with different experiences than our own. The more we sur round ourselves with diverse perspectives, the greater the likelihood that we'll arrive at solutions—solutions we could not materialize on our own. Put simply, diversity of experiences, thoughts and perspectives is foundational for maximiz ing creativity and innovation. Without different ways of viewing problems and situations (and people with an open minded approach to new ideas and perspec tives) we stifle creativity and innovation. Diversity and inclusion are naturally linked to creativity and innovation.

The question becomes, "Is creativity and innovation important to your organi zation?" If not, then from a business perspective there's not much need to work on issues of diversity and inclusion. But if creativity and innovation are crucial to becoming "better, stronger, and faster" and staying ahead of the competition, then the work of diversity and inclusion is not an option. It is an imperative.

As we continue the transition from an industrial age based on manufacturing to a creative era centered on knowledge, the importance of creativity and in novation only will increase. In the 21st century, ideas matter. In fact, one might say, "Ideas Rule!" Are you limiting your organization's ability to generate novel ideas by limiting your diversity? Likewise, are you limiting the strength of the diversity you may have by asking for sameness and assimilation or by requir ing uniformity in the search for unity? If you don not find ways to genuinely include, value and engage your employees and allow their unique contributions, you are possibly smothering the next break through innovation? The work of diversity and inclusion is vital to maximizing creativity and innovation. Are you doing that work well? In a world of diversity and multiple perspectives and back grounds, harmony is difficult to come by when everyone is required to sing the same note.

I must confess that it will take some time and intentional work on my part before my beloved tape loses its top of mind position as the premier solution to all things broken. Some things just get stuck (again, pun intended) in our heads. Developing a diversity and inclusion mindset is hard work, but it's necessary if we are to operate smoothly in an increasingly diverse world where ideas matter where creativity and innovation are the hallmarks of great organizations, and those that will be around for a long time!

To know and yet think we do not know is the highest attainment. Not to know
and yet think we do know is a disease.
~ Lao tzu ~

4

Cognitive Collections

LET it be known that I, being in good standing in the brotherhood of men,
freely and willfully, under no physical, psychological or spiritual duress, de
clare publicly my love for minivans. Yes, I understand this essentially voids my
"Men's Club" membership, but there are times when one must humbly admit, "I
had it all wrong."

Like many who have ample supplies of testosterone, I am genetically predis
posed to scorn minivans. It has been only in the past few years that I discovered
a hidden but unmistakable affection for a vehicle that my DNA does not hold in
high regard. This was not a sudden revelatory flash, like the kind I get when food
does not play well with my digestive tract and I scurry for the nearest bathroom.
No, it's more like the gradual recognition that having kids is punishment for
once being a kid.

When minivans first arrived on the market, I wondered who possibly could
have designed such an eyesore? The bigger question though is, "Who were the
intellectual giants that let the design get past concept stage...and what drugs were
they on?" In my eyes, minivans were only one automotive evolutionary step
above the AMC Pacer. If you dare picture a Pacer in your mind (and I am not re
sponsible for what might happen thereafter) you might notice that it looks eerily
similar to vehicles that transport dead people.

Truly, the Pacer was a stunningly unique idea for an automobile. I can picture
the scene in which the Pacer hatched into a concept. It's a smoke-filled, dimly

lit room deep in the AMC product development dungeons of Detroit. Around a big table sits a bunch of research and design folks who failed to break the gravitational pull of the 60's. They all look alike. Each is wearing a tie dyed button down shirt, accented with a fashionable 1970's orange, clip on tie. In an historical "aha" moment, one of these fine gentlemen launches from his seat and exclaims, "Let's build something that would redefine the term 'ugly car' and try to sell it." Thus, the drug-induced birth of the AMC Pacer. Okay, okay, minivans aren't that bad, but it's not a big leap to see how homo Paceris (at least early ver sions) is genetically linked to modern day homo Minivanis.

Suffice it to say, I once had many negative perceptions and attitudes towards minivans, and who could blame me. I remember reading a report that confirmed my negativity. From what I can recall, the research basically said that when a man and a woman are in the front seats of a four door sedan, the man is driv ing 80 percent of the time. But when it comes to minivans, the percentages switched...the woman drives 80 percent of the time! It had been ingrained that minivans were for the more feminine of the species homo erectus.

I only had one cognitive folder in which I stored all my information about minivans. Any data was thrown into that one folder. When I saw anything that resembled a minivan, that information went into the folder. Chrysler minivans, Ford minivans, Honda minivans...they all looked the same to me. I never really got inside any of the minivans, so I never saw their unique features and person alities. If I had taken a closer look, I might have created sub folders for Chrysler or Ford minivans, within the general "Minivan" folder. But I didn't, because to me, a minivan of any make was a minivan for women.

And then it happened, an experience so powerful that it began to change my thinking about the world (mostly the part about minivans). My wife and I had a kid...then two and three and before I knew it we had four. As parents know, adding children to your life brings with it tons of stuff: A Pack n Play, car seats, toys, diaper bags, clothes, etc. And when you go on any type of overnight trip, that "stuff" comes along. Now, lugging around baby stuff in a four-door sedan wasn't too bad with one child, and we still managed with two kids. But when child number three was on the way, I came to the dreadful realization that a mini van would park in our garage and that my friends would see me in it...or worse, that they would see me driving it.

I brainstormed alternatives. "Leaving a kid or two behind to fend for them selves when we go on trips might work," I thought, but then those pesky people from Child Protective Services enter the picture. Following my wife in our sedan while she drives the minivan seemed wasteful and expensive. Disguising myself looked like more work than its worth. In the end, all my calculations produced the same answer: A minivan was in my future.

My future route foreseen, I began to take notice of minivans when I saw them on the street. I paid attention to minivan ads in magazines and on TV. I sought out research reporting all the wonderful benefits of minivans. Soon, I could dif ferentiate one minivan from another. I could tell which ones got a five-star rating on a crash test and which ones didn't. How much horsepower does a Ford Wind star have? I knew that. I knew which models were "sporty" and which ones were "luxury," although the phrase "luxury minivan" struck me as an oxymoron, like "gourmet take-out."

I knew there was no turning back when I test-drove my first minivan. I was expecting a clunky, school bus type ride, but what I experienced felt better than most sedans I'd driven. I test drove many minivans, even the ones I knew I wouldn't buy, just for the fun of it. Once I got behind the wheel of some mini vans, I began to like them. At first, I admired their great utility. Later, I could see how the words "luxury" and "minivan" found each other. Children aside, I was sold on minivans. So today, my cognitive minivan folder is filled with many sub folders. I have a Honda subfolder, a Ford subfolder, a Chrysler subfolder, a Nissan subfolder, etc. I can see how minivans are distinct from each other and how each model has something that sets it apart.

How many cognitive folders do you have when it comes to people, especially people different than you? Do you have just one or do you have many. Do you have sub-folders labeled "Mexican" and "Chicano" and "Puerto Rican?" Or do you lump everyone whom you perceive as Hispanic/Latino into one main folder, and think about them all the same way? Do an evaluation of your cognitive fold ers. Do some of your main folders have more sub folders than others? Is there a diversity of folders that help you interpret and explain situations and interactions from multiple perspectives? Or do your folders narrow your view of people?

If you have myriad sub folders, is the information correct and complete? It's a good thing to ask yourself where you got the information in your folders, and how balanced it is. Did it come from indirect sources (i.e., television), that might also have incomplete or incorrect folders, or did it come from real, direct and balanced interaction with different people? It is said that you can only know what you know. Likewise, your people folders and sub folders are limited to the experiences you've had. In an ever changing world, it's good to have lots of folders and sub folders about people. The more good information we have, the greater the chance we'll make good decisions when interacting with others.

It took a while for me to get my minivan folders and sub folders in shape. In fact, they still are evolving. Each year, I look forward to the introduction of new minivan models so I can enhance my neural network of minivan folders. Do you look forward to meeting and interacting with new, different people so you can grow your network of people folders? If you do, that's great. Do you put yourself in positions that allow you to create new sub folders? If you do, that's awesome! A curiosity about people and the world, coupled with an open mindedness to entertain new perspectives, is a powerful combination in an increasingly diverse and complex world. Do you have this combination? Are you intentionally work ing to get it, or make it stronger? And are you modeling it to others, especially kids?

I just found out that there's a new minivan coming out that has a 260 horse power, V6 motor, 21 cup holders and a 60/40 split rear seat with passenger win dows that "roll" down. How cool is that? They're also talking about making a four wheel drive version. Now there's a minivan for me!

The voyage of discovery is not in seeking new landscapes
but in having new eyes.
~ Marcel Proust~

5
A New Search Routine

THERE is a chorus that rings incessantly through our house. Once benign background noise, it now evokes a response that generally requires anger man agement therapy. Those with children, or those who spend much of their time near children, probably know the haunting words, "Where's my Gameboy game?"

I bought this thing called a Gameboy several years ago for my oldest son, Nicholas. At the time I was unaware of the troubles it would bring. What I thought was a cool, electronic toy that hip dads buy their kids has turned into a frequent source of mental and emotional frustration.

It's really not my fault. I just can't resist when palm sized gizmos blink their sexy red and green LED's at me. What I hear is an unrelenting cry to release them from their paper and plastic prisons to do what they were meant to do. "Free me, free me," they say, and I can't just walk away from their pleas for lib erty. How can anyone ignore a Gameboy's inalienable right to be a Gameboy?

Looking back, I can see how my genetic predisposition to all high tech gad gets clouded my ordinarily strong decision making skills (images of my wife laughing play profusely in my head). Yeah, I know it sounds overly dramatic but sometimes you to have to rationalize bad decisions.

Anyway, the Gameboy entered our home. There were few problems at first, primarily because Nicholas only had one game cartridge. To clarify, when you buy a Gameboy unit you also have to get game cartridges at additional cost. When there is only one game cartridge, it is always in the unit, and presumably can't get lost. But here lies the real problem with Gameboys. When you have more than one game cartridge, the ones that aren't plugged into the Gameboy often get misplaced. And when they are lost, the increasingly annoying chorus rings out, "Where's my Gameboy game?"

Nicholas quickly learned the words after getting his second Gameboy game cartridge. The refrain was acceptable at first...as a solo. But in another lapse of judgment, I purchased our second oldest son, Zachary, a Gameboy. So, be cause of my inability to keep my hi tech hormones in check, my wife and I hear "Where's my Gameboy game" in two-part harmony.

The initial annoyance was offset by the surreal peace and quiet that visited us on long road trips. From a parent's perspective, there are few things more heavenly than looking in your rear view mirror to see two of your kids quietly enjoying each other's company. No fighting. No screaming. No noise. Just two precious little children wasting away their little brains in the mesmerizing light of a Pokemon game. Gives me virtual goose bumps just thinking about it.

Of course, home is where all the problems arise. And to be fair, it's not really the Gameboys that are the problem, it's the kids who play them. Because we all know that Gameboys don't kill parents, kids do. Here is a recent exchange be tween my sons and me that illustrates the pain Gameboys can cause. It had been a quiet, relaxing evening, allowing my wife and I to spend some time with one another...the daily 10 minute, quality time typical of U.S. couples. And then it starts.

Running up the stairs, Zachary asks, "Where's my Gameboy game?"

"I don't know. Where did you put it?" I fire back. "Which one are you looking for?"

"I can't find Pokemon Silver Version. I looked everywhere." Frustration floods through his words.

"And I can't find Pokemon Ruby Version," Nicholas chimes in.

"I suppose you looked everywhere, too?"

"Yep, Zachary and I looked in all the places we've played our Gameboys. We looked in our room, the toy room and the car. We looked everywhere," Nicholas says without truly grasping the meaning of the word "everywhere."

"How about Jacob's room, or Natalie's room or the back room?" I ask with decreasing patience.

Confidently, Zachary says, "Our games aren't in those places. We never play them there."

I commended Zachary on his use of logic, but then told him that I saw his little sister Natalie playing in her room with something that looked very much like a Gameboy game cartridge. Still confident that the game cartridges can't be in places where he never plays them, Zachary insists, "I know they're not there."

Breaking a string of bad Gameboy related decisions, I look at Zachary and Nicholas and say, "Let's go look in Natalie's room."

As we walk in, the boys make a quick scan of the room. "See, I told ya, dad!" Zachary exclaims. "They aren't in here." Nicholas says nothing, continuing to look.

"Look harder, Zach, like your brother's doing."

Reluctantly, Zachary makes a more thorough investigation of the room. He and Nicholas look under Natalie's chairs, behind her dresser, by her crib...no Gameboy game cartridges.

"See, I told ya," Zachary says again. "They're not here."

"Check in the corner, behind her crib," I tell them.

Nicholas takes a peek. "Here they are!" he exclaims. "And there's more than the Pokemon games. Here's the F 14 Fighter game you've been looking for, Zach."

I look at Zachary, trying to suppress an "I told you so," but I can't. So I just say it. Sometimes you have to revert to a snotty, 6 year old mentality to deal with snotty, 6 year olds. (Don't tell my wife that.) Zachary gives me an innocent smile and says, "It's not our fault we couldn't find the games at first. They've never been in Natalie's room. We've never had to look there before. They've always been downstairs."

With a stash of Gameboy game cartridges in hand, Nicholas and Zachary rush out of Natalie's room. No "thanks for the help dad" or anything of that sort to hint of any gratitude. Aren't they supposed to teach these manner type things at school? Then, as I leave my little girl's room, Zachary comes around the corner, gives me a hug and says "thanks dad for showing us another place to look for our games when they get lost." Ahh, all is now right in the world of parenting.

It you haven't picked it up yet, there is a teachable moment here for those who may have some reservations about affirmative action, in terms of hiring and promotion. However you define affirmative action, it has, in concept, always encouraged us to look in places that have been off our radar screen. It's about "forcing" us to do things that we should have been doing in the first place, espe cially in a country that prides itself on equality and justice.

If you and your organization want to find the best people representing diverse experiences and perspectives, then you must search in new places, places you've never even thought of searching. My sons were unable to find their Gameboy cartridges until they searched in a new place. Their regular routine often had been successful, but became outdated when their little sister started moving around. Now they have to search other places in the house, opening the doors of many rooms.

In an increasingly diverse environment, your quest for "diverse" candidates and employees requires you to consider more than just the doors that you've always used. Door #1 and door #2 may have produced good, "qualified" employ ees for you in the past, and likely will do so in the future. But don't be blind to doors #3, #4, #5 and #6 (which have always existed). Progressive, enlightened organizations committed to diversity and inclusion (read: maybe your competi tors) will be looking behind those doors. And they will find some of the best and brightest in the places you've been overlooking.

If you are committed and intentional about changing your search routine, you will find that "disabled" people are not as disabled as you think they are. Or that "Asians" know more much more than math, and that some aren't even math oriented. You might discover, God forbid, that many women are extraor dinary leaders who would outdo many men if given the opportunity. How might your organization be enriched if you opened some new doors and found that older people still tick with great fervor beyond age 65? Or that a Morehead State graduate can outshine a Harvard alum? And what if people with non European accents have talents and skills that extend beyond the shop floor?

Doors unopened are opportunities unclaimed. Once you decide to seek the benefits behind untouched doors, don't just open the door for a quick scan like my sons did. Stay a while and make a thorough search, and do it with sincerity. The people you seek may need to get better acquainted with you before they decide it's "safe" to connect. Reaching out to audiences that harbor suspicion (because you were never there before) will require a sustained effort. It's often a matter of trust, and one "help wanted" posting in an "ethnic" newspaper usually doesn't cut it. It's just one small step in the journey that builds trust in communi ties that historically have been neglected.

By making sincere, ongoing efforts to look in places you've never looked before, you are taking "affirming action." If more people and organizations took affirming action, there would be little need to have affirmative action policies. Such policies, still necessary, stem from a history of legal and societal doors being slammed in the face of people who were the "wrong" race, gender, age, religion, etc.

If you happened to be part of an unfortunate group that was the "wrong" (fill in the blank), you were often dismissed without even a chance to compete. And to make matters worse, you were labeled "unqualified" by people who are unen lightened about your great potential, and they say things like "we have to find a qualified (fill in the blank)." The underlying assumption is that you, and others like you, are very few in number, and so it is difficult finding "qualified ones."

It will take time, energy and commitment to change hiring and promotion strategies that tend to be ineffective in the face of increasing diversity. It will require those who are truly committed to a level playing field (where everyone at least gets a tryout) to examine and, likely, change their attitudes, beliefs and behavioral practices. Making that commitment to change to recognize and open other doors - is the very essence of "affirming action." With that approach we would not need legally-based affirmative action.

So there are two roads before us: Internally motivated "affirming action" or externally influenced affirmative action. Which road do you choose?

There are risks and costs to a program of action, but they are far less than the long range risks and costs of comfortable inaction.
~ President John F. Kennedy ~

6
A Late Start

AFTER nearly 25 years of telling myself, "I wish I could play the guitar," I actually am trying to learn how. It's part of my strategic life plan to every now and then inject inner turmoil via a new endeavor. Four months after buying my first guitar, I find the life plan is working out quite well; inner turmoil and I are good friends at the moment.

Playing the guitar looks so easy...when someone else is doing it. My inaccu rate perception of the skills it takes to play the guitar is a significant reason I put off learning for so long. I mistakenly believed that I could just "pick it up" at any time. "Guess again buddy," say the guitar gods.

If you didn't know, the guitar gods are a group of beings that oversee, you guessed it, guitars and guitar playing. They make up the guitar rules to which everyone is bound. They are the ones who decided there would be six strings on a guitar (though they later passed an amendment allowing twelve strings). They also ordained that anyone who seeks guitar enlightenment will endure months of raw, painful fingertips followed by a loss of feeling anything with those same fingertips...for the rest of one's life, and maybe beyond.

To fill the guitar-playing world with people of utmost dedication, the guitar gods made the process of learning the art as painful as possible, and early on de clared that all guitar strings would be made out of steel. They later had to allow nylon string guitars because too many people were cutting their fingers on the steel strings (some were even slicing up their arms when a string would pop), and they were running out of people to whom they could be guitar gods.

Initially, to convert non players, the guitar gods made guitar playing fairly simple, though still painful. Any and all songs could be played with five chords: C, D, E, G and A. With just a little practice, the finger placements required by these chords are relatively easy to master. But they found that less than worthy folks (like politicians) were taking up the guitar and creating imbalance in the guitar universe. They could not let that happen, so they created new, evil chords like B and F sharp, and the most evil chords of all, bar chords. The initial difficulty of these chords stopped many folks in their tracks. The people could not understand why these new chords, which require a guitarist to be double jointed and have the grip strength of an actor turned governor, were necessary. But they endured the pain and discomfort. With fewer politicians and more worthy people now playing the guitar, balance once again visited the realm of the guitar gods.

Many hear the call to play the guitar, but only a few are chosen. Of course, I want to be among the chosen. I've wanted membership for a long time and actually pursued it several times, though half heartedly. I never fully committed, and as a result I am currently trying to jump the B and F chord hurdles with painfully slow success. Even with this momentary stall, I intend to show my worth to the guitar gods. This time, I will not stop. I will not fail. I will not take shortcuts. I am not a politician.

But I admit it is tough to maneuver my fingers into the proper positioning for chords such as B or even Bm. Approaching my 40s, I found out that certain appendages on my body do not work with exacting precision as they once did. Now before your mind wanders too far, I am talking about my hands. They do not always do what I want them to do, at least not very well. I'm not sure if the signals sent from my brain are a bit corrupted, or if my hands are passive aggressively getting back at me after years of blistering them up as a youngster playing tennis. Either way, it's taking much longer to learn to play at even the simplest level, and the dexterity I had in younger days has locked itself in some safety box to which my brain has lost the key.

I knew from the very beginning of this process that buying a nice, expensive guitar would motivate me to endure the tough times. So I did, and it has helped. It's tougher just to give up when you've made a substantial investment. And as it turns out, once you purchase a guitar, the guitar gods, through some vexing spell, direct you to invest in guitar related paraphernalia.

After the initial guitar purchase, I could not keep myself from taking frequent trips to the local guitar shop, always leaving with something in hand. Since my guitar was an "acoustic-electric," meaning it could be directly plugged into an amplifier, I was compelled to purchase, yes, an amplifier. And since you need a cord to connect the guitar to the amplifier, I had to buy a cord. Oh yes, and that amplifier I bought has an additional input for a microphone, so one day I walked out of the guitar shop with...right again, a microphone and the necessary cord. Additional trips equipped me with an electronic tuner, assorted picks, guitar books and DVDs that teach you how to play (they really don't, but it sounded good at the time), a music stand, a microphone stand, a stand for my guitar, a stand for my amplifier, a stand for the stand of my amplifier, Custard's last stand...you get the picture.

Going to the guitar shop got a bit time consuming, so I started buying things online. The World Wide Web makes it much more convenient to empty my bank account. Getting into the guitar world is an expensive, never ending process of obtaining more equipment (kind of like golf, but that's another story). I suspect that the guitar gods are angel investors in many of the guitar shops around the world, and now hold significant equity stake in these places. But I rationalized all these purchases, er, investments...with a philosophy similar to that of Billy Crystal's character Fernando from Saturday Night Live, "It is better to look good than to play good." And look good, I do. Is there anything sexier than a little Asian guy strapped with a guitar about half his size surrounded by a mountain of stands? Didn't think so.

Okay, back to reality. I often have wondered how well I might be playing the guitar right now if I had started learning as a teenager. I'm sure I would have mastered it quickly. I had much more on my side then   more time, more nimble fingers and more motivation (I was under the impression that no matter how unsightly you might be, you could get girls if you played the guitar...kind of like Willie Nelson). I would have saved a lot of money by starting earlier as well, primarily because at that time I didn't have much money to spend on all the guitar stuff that was available, which is probably just a fraction of the equipment available today. But here I am more than two decades later struggling to fix my fingers into positions not meant for human hands. Nonetheless, I press on (pun intended) because if I don't start now, I'll be writing a similar story 10 years from now. Wouldn't that be a shame?

With my late start on the guitar in mind, I ask you how your diversity initiatives are coming along, if at all. Have you and your organization made a full commitment to persevere, even when tough hurdles arise? Do you have lots of things you have wanted to do, but just haven't?

I recently was part of a discussion that touched on the idea of "growing our own." In the particular community where this discussion took place, many commented that the "lack of diversity" made it very difficult to attract and retain professionals of color. A person in the discussion group said her company had the idea more than 10 years ago to engage children of color while they were still in junior high school, to introduce them to the business and teach them about a profession that continues to lack people of color and women. Others chimed in saying they had the same idea, but never truly pursued it. I asked what it might be like today if they had committed to a "grow our own" initiative. All were silent for a moment but you could tell they were thinking, "What if?"

Okay, so you have some good ideas, but haven't started. What are you going to do about it now with the unstoppable thrust of a more diverse world in your face? What if you start now? Could you be reaping the rewards in a few years? It might take longer than that but you'll never know if you don't start...with full commitment.

"I coulda been a contenda," if only I would have started playing the guitar years ago. How will your organization contend in the future if you don't take a serious look at diversity and inclusion issues now? If yours is one of those orga nizations that fully committed years ago, congratulations. You have a big head start on many. If you are still spinning your wheels, I suggest you start putting your ideas into action. Playing the guitar is still a matter of choice for me. Being a diverse, inclusive and culturally competent organization is no longer a choice for organizations, it is an imperative.

How good at "diversity and inclusion" could you be in five years if you start ed in earnest today? With continued blessings from the guitar gods, I plan to play the guitar well in five years. I'm passionate about the guitar. I have an unwavering commitment to play well. And I have made a substantial financial investment. Can you and your organization say similar things when it comes to diversity and inclusion?

*Treat people as if they were what they should be, and you help them become
what they are capable of becoming.*
~ Johan von Goethe ~

7
Wanted: Good Role Models

I dread it when my wife cooks. At least, I used to. And it's not because she's
a bad cook. Far from it. She makes the kinds of meals that force me to go on two
diets…because one diet doesn't give me enough food. No, I don't like it when
my wife cooks because, in addition to the tasty dishes she makes, she has this
thing about health and nutrition that compels her to prepare these things called
vegetables. The very existence of vegetables, especially green ones, proves there
is a God with a twisted sense of humor. How else do you explain that a class of
foods required for a healthy body also makes taste buds curl up and die on con
tact? As you see, I am not a big vegetable lover   and I don't like little vegetables,
either.   I tried to find some fondness in my stomach for them, and even devel
oped a working relationship with potatoes, corn and cucumbers. But just when I
started to think that vegetables were not the reason for the existence of our gag
reflex, I found out that the three I enjoy are not technically vegetables.

So where did I get my disdain for vegetables? Well, my guess is that it comes
from a lack of positive history with vegetables. I did not eat many of them grow
ing up, or if I did, I have suppressed most of those traumatic episodes. I do have a
rather upsetting recollection of my mother forcing me to eat some spinach when
I was 7 years old. I tried to resist, the way kids have resisted for ages, by holding
the spinach in my mouth for a few hours without swallowing. That, it turns out,
is a bad strategy since spinach, like other vegetables, doesn't exactly get better
tasting after a lengthy soak in saliva. Also, a war of attrition is not a good idea

when your opponent is a woman whose cultural heritage is known for unflinch
ing patience.

It had been a while since I felt compelled to eat vegetables, but somehow
parental responsibilities have a way of making me do things I'd rather not do.
For example, on occasion I like to let out a loud burp, which is a very acceptable
thing to do if you're French. It's the French way of showing satisfaction with a
meal, and I have a connection with the French. I grew up Catholic, and if you're
up on Vietnamese history, you would know that French Catholics had a signifi
cant influence on Vietnam. So, as a result of the work of Catholic missionaries,
I enjoy burping. Who says missionaries have little impact?

Anyway, with kids around, I can't just go around burping any time I wish. As
a parent I have learned that kids like to do things they see their parents doing. So,
if I constantly burp with pride in front of my kids, I shouldn't be surprised to see
them doing the same thing, at home or in public. To help my kids grow up in a
healthy, acceptable manner, I have to be careful about what I model to them.
And this is where we come back to the vegetables. Here is a classic example of
how a perfectly great dinner can be ruined by displaying parental leadership.

The family is sitting around the table eagerly awaiting some tasty lasagna.
My wife makes great lasagna (any of you who get the pleasure of meeting my
wife need to reiterate this point). Her lasagna is great because of the ingredients
she uses. Of course, the star ingredient in lasagna is the meat, not the noodles or
tomato sauce or whatever else might not be full of fat and cholesterol. (Cheese,
since it has been linked to obesity, clogged arteries and, in high dosages, doesn't
do much for extending one's life, also is an important ingredient. Any true carni
vore knows the attributes of real food.) As I fill my plate with the meaty compo
nents of the lasagna, I observe, out of the corner of my eye, an appetite reducing
move by my wife. She places a steaming dish of green beans on the table, right
in front of me. What had I done to deserve this? I run the good husband checklist
through my head: I took out the trash this week, I have said "I love you" numer
ous times and it has been a while since I walked into a small room with her,
closed the door and flatulated. Where had I gone wrong?

Trying to ignore the green beans, I dig into my lasagna. I slowly look up to see
green beans on all my kids' plates, then quickly return to my meaty dish. Then
son number three, Jacob, says to me, "Hey dad, aren't you going to have some
green beans?" I knew we should have stopped at two kids.

"I'm not that hungry tonight, Jacob. What I have on my plate is all I need."

Zachary, the second oldest, rings in, "You should have some, dad. Mom says
they'll make you big and strong." An only child would have been nice, I fanta
sized.

The leader of this pack of kids, Nicholas, senses my vulnerability and swoops
in for the kill, "Yeah, dad, if we have to have them you have to have them,
too."

Now I have no choice. Nicholas has played the "be a good role model" card. Dreadfully, I scoop a few green beans onto my plate. "That's only three," Jacob jumps in. "Have more, dad. They're good for you." I put some more green beans onto my plate and keep eating my lasagna. I wished we had a dog or some other animal that I might secretly feed the beans, but accepting the fact that I have to be an omnivore in this family, I eventually clear my plate. I guess this is what it means to be a good parent, a good role model. If I want my kids to eat healthy foods like vegetables, I also must do it. I have to model behaviors I expect in my children.

How are you doing at modeling inclusive and culturally competent behavior to others around you, whether it is your kids, friends or co workers? If you are in leadership, are you mindful of what you are teaching and affirming in others through your actions? What do you do when you hear a demeaning joke? What action do you take when you recognize non majority voices are not being heard? Do you want people in your organiza tion to attend cultural competence training? Are you willing to go first?

If you want your kids to respect and engage different perspectives, do you let them see you doing those things? Telling your kids (or anyone else) is not as powerful as showing them that it's good to have relationships with people who see the world differently than you. Behavioral messages are much more compel ling than verbal messages, and when the two conflict, in more cases than not, the walk overpowers the talk. I get a kick out of parents who, after finding out that their kids have shown disrespect to someone who is "different," say something like, "We don't teach our kids prejudice." or "My kids don't learn that at home." Sometimes the question is not what we are actively teaching kids, but what kids are subtly learning from our actions, or lack of actions.

If you want your kids or others to look at you for leadership in diversity and inclusion (or any other area), are you truly willing to engage in the same process of learning and experiencing that you want for them? Do you have close friends that are "different" than you? Are you willing to feel initial discomfort to explore realities different than your own? Can you entertain new ideas, new perspectives and new ways of doing things with an open mind and positive attitude? These are some of the attributes of a culturally competent person, attributes that are getting more important as our nation grows more diverse.

I may not like to eat vegetables or refrain from burping in front of my kids, but I know that it's in their best interest   and mine, too   to model those behav iors. If I don't actively teach them the "right stuff," then I must accept that I have a part in any unwanted behavior they display in the future.

Over the course of time I have grown to like some of the vegetables my wife and kids have "forced" me to eat. I'm just hoping that no one bursts my bubble one day by informing me that carrots and spinach are not vegetables.

It is a great shock at the age of five or six to find that in a world of Gary Coopers you are the Indian.
~ James Baldwin ~

8
Harmless Images?

AN American Indian friend of mine once told me a story that I find enlighten ing, especially for those of us with children. You see, my friend has an 8 year old son who enjoys watching cowboy and "Indian" movies on television.

Before the start of a show, the little boy would dress up in traditional Ameri can Indian clothing, proudly putting on the authentic garments his grandmother had made for him. Of course, he also would get something to snack on before he plopped down in front of the screen; he didn't miss a moment of these shows.

The father, pleased that his son would wear traditional Native dress, didn't pay attention to the content of the programs at first. He soon would take notice.

One day, the father came home to find his son watching another cowboy and "Indian" program. As usual, his son sat not more than three feet from the televi sion munching some chips. But this time, something looked different. Instead of Native clothing, the boy was wearing a cowboy hat and a bandana around his neck. A plastic rifle was at his side where he usually clutched a play bow-and-ar row.

My friend walked over to his son and began, "Son, usually when you watch these shows you dress in our Native clothing. I am so proud when you do that. Why are you dressed like this today, like a cowboy?"

The little boy looked at his dad and matter of factly said, "Sometimes, I wan na win too, Dad."

When I heard this story, I was struck with sadness. I couldn't help but think of how these cowboy and "Indian" shows affected the little boy's psyche and self esteem, and how they continue to mold the minds of all children (and adults) who watch them.

Viewing these types of programs over and over again, as the little boy did, gradually develops images in our heads about who are "winners" and who are "losers," about who is superior and who is inferior.

Sadly, shows like this still intrigue us as they did a whole generation of people who are now adults. And most people who watch them never have had any sig nificant, meaningful interaction with an American Indian! So, many of the im ages of American Indians in our society, how we view them and think of them, have come from indirect sources   often based on incomplete, inaccurate and biased information.

Whether we learned it from television, teachers, faith institutions, storybooks or even parents, the way we box American Indians in our heads is likely more stereotype than reality, more myth than truth.

As I said, there is now a whole generation of adults who grew up watching shows that portrayed American Indians and other people of color in stereotypi cally negative roles with off putting characteristics. Undoubtedly, many of these adults carry images about American Indians that reflect the stock characters they saw on television or read about in books.

We all must challenge ourselves to get the "truth, the whole truth and nothing but the truth" about American Indians. Only then might we begin to understand why many people take offense at schools with "Indian" mascots."

Be less certain. Be more curious.
~ Steve L. Robbins ~

9
Strange New Worlds

QUESTION: Do you know which television program was one of the first to receive a lot of recognition for its diversity? If you said Star Trek, you're right. In many ways, it went where no show had gone before.

Imagine with me for a moment Captain James T. Kirk's crew on the U.S.S. Starship Enterprise. Zero in on the captain's deck. Do you notice the racial and ethnic diversity? Indeed, for 1960s television, there was substantial diversity. Can you see it? Behind and just to the left of the captain's chair is Lieutenant Uhura instant messaging other Federation Starships with her little earphone. Toward the front sits Lieutenant Chekov piloting the Enterprise to strange new worlds. Can you picture Sulu? He was doing something technical, I'm sure.

Then, of course, you had the big cheese himself, Captain Kirk. Perched in his chair looking at the vast screen before him, you know he's wondering when he will get his next chance to break the Prime Directive. And next to him is the Vulcan, Spock, who seals the deal. You know you have diversity when you have an alien, legal or not.

Scurrying around the engine room is Scotty, working to squeeze just a little more warp speed out of the Dylithium crystals, hoping they don't blow. And Bones is in the sick room rehearsing another way to tell Kirk that he's only a doctor.

It's easy to see why many saw Star Trek as a model of diversity, especially for its time. In its era, the program stood alone for its progressive attempts to represent a universe of diversity. Some people might argue that the original Star

Trek series still surpasses many modern shows with respect to racial and ethnic inclusion.

However, another perspective sees the diversity of Star Trek differently. Throw away the previous images in your head, and let's examine the show through another lens. Let's look at it with an eye for hierarchy (read: power and privilege distribution), from the top on down.

Let's begin with a few questions. Who was the Captain of the Starship Enter prise? Who was the Chief Engineer? Who was the Chief Medical Officer? Are you starting to see a pattern? If you are thinking, "white guys" you have the correct lens on.

Look further. Who was the First Officer? Yes, he was half alien, but his other half was...yes, half white guy! Now, for you white men reading this, this does not mean that "white guys" are bad or that you should not be leaders. It is merely an observation of the facts. And the observation prompts a logical question: "Is any organization, any community, any nation, any spaceship any anything at its best in an increasingly diverse world when its leadership is more or less ho mogeneous?"

In a 21st century world where creativity and innovation (read: ideas) may be the only edge over competitors, similarity and uniformity (and the expectation of similarity and uniformity) place difficult barriers on the road to creativity and innovation. Why? Simply put, if the maximization of creativity and innovation depends on a rich diversity of perspectives, then groups and organizations that are populated by people too similar in attitudes, approaches and actions will find themselves limited – slowed by the bounds of impulse power while others race ahead using the warp drives of diversity and inclusion.

From a hierarchical perspective, Star Trek was not at all diverse. In fact, as a friend of mine, who examines the show from a different perspective, half jok ingly puts it, "Star Trek wasn't a show about diversity, it was just the another show about a middle aged white guy sitting in a big easy chair watching a big screen TV telling people what to do." If you laughed a little here, you are well on your way to understanding another key ingredient in the stew of creativity and innovation (ingredient one being a diversity of perspectives) which is an open ness to different perspectives.

Let me be clear that an openness to different ideas and perspectives does not necessarily mean you must accept them. It simply means you have a willingness to entertain and understand a perspective different than your own. If you didn't laugh, well, you are the very person for which this book was written.

Humor aside, these two simple ways of looking at Star Trek illustrate how people from different perspectives can view the same set of "facts" and come away with very different interpretations. Neither is necessarily right or wrong; each interpretation is valid from a particular perspective, with a particular lens. The problem is that there are often multiple valid perspectives, yet not enough people willing to entertain those perspectives that do not comfortably fit within their own limited frameworks of reality.

Every day, we constantly interpret information. And we do so based on a set of lenses generated by our past encounters and experiences. A definition of culture by sociologist James Spradley underscores this simply and succinctly, "Culture is the acquired knowledge people use to interpret experience and gen erate behavior." It is not a big stretch to understand how different people, with different experiences and lenses, can interpret the same information quite differ ently.

The existence of different perspectives and interpretations in any given situ ation is not necessarily good or bad. However, we run into problems when we convince ourselves that our own interpretation, our own perspective, is the cor rect one and that all others are flawed. "We must be right," we tell ourselves! But our tunnel vision often blinds us to opportunities literally sitting in our midst, made invisible by our inflexible worldview. When we are unwilling to hear or experience perspectives different than our own, we lose the potential richness of multiple, diverse perspectives. We short change ourselves of possible solutions to vexing problems   solutions that often are reached only when diverse view points are considered, mixed and allowed to warm our thoughts.

So, how tolerant are you of different perspectives? How willing are you to look through another lens? Your level of tolerance to different ideas, especially those that might initially make you uncomfortable, will have a direct impact on how you operate in an increasingly diverse world, where multiple approaches, ideas and ways of doing things are vital to long term success.

So go ahead, take a voyage to explore strange new worlds. Make it your ongoing mission to boldly go to places (physical and mental) you have never gone before. Break the Prime Directive and get involved in the lives of those you found alien in the past. It may be uncomfortable, even painful for a time. But, after a while you will most likely enjoy your new journey. If you allow, the journey will transform your thinking. It will birth a new you—a humble, open minded person with the courage to entertain the exciting unpredictability that novelty brings. And imagine what might happen if the "starship", uh, orga nization you are in was filled with people like that. The possibilities are endless. Ready to turn on the warp drives? Then make it so! And live long and prosper my friend.

"Once we rid ourselves of traditional thinking we can get on with creating the future."
~ James Bertrand ~

10
Equal Not Always Fair

A few years ago I attended a conference held in one of my favorite cities, Chi cago. It was a crisp and beautiful fall day, a lazy wind blowing colorful leaves everywhere I looked. After checking in to my downtown hotel and finding my room I, like always, explored the grounds. As I walked the halls looking for the fitness area (healthy living always begins with good intentions) busily checking voice mail with my cell phone, I entered what I thought was the men's restroom. I immediately noticed something wrong; I could find no urinals on the wall. Five stalls, but no urinals. And the clinching telltale sign, this place I thought was the men's restroom smelled rather nice.

Immediately after realizing this was not where a person of my packaged goods should be, I quickly left. Fortunately, no one observed my mindless, cell phone enabled mistake.

I went across the hall to the men's restroom and, comforted by the urinals on the wall, did what I set out to do. On my way out, I noticed there were three wall urinals and two stalls. "Those architects who designed these buildings must be enlightened about gender equity," I thought, comparing the five places for relief in the women's restroom and the five places in the men's restroom. Feeling good about the state of gender equity regarding restrooms, I retired to my room cell phone turned off for a good night's rest.

The conference began the next day with a great opening session during which everyone seemed to have a cup, or two or three, of coffee or tea. At break time, there was the expected rush of people in search of restrooms. Some people fired up their cell phones as they searched. "Big mistake," I thought.

I, too, had to use the restroom and I knew exactly where it was. As I approached the men's room, I looked back across the hall. A big line had formed at the entrance to the women's restroom. I then looked to where I was headed. There was no line, and no wait at my restroom. Yes!

Feeling a little guilty about my immediate relief, I thought about what I had observed. Long line for women. No line for men. Hmmm. "This might not be fair," my inner voice of justice and equality whispered.

I thought about those architects who designed the building and my recent sense of satisfaction with restroom equality. The architects, most likely male, had done the "equal" thing. Five relief places for women, five relief places for men. At first glance, it seems like the right thing to do, conceptually.

But the break in the conference exposed a different operational reality. Treating people "equally" is not necessarily the same as treating people "fairly." Without going into too much detail, let's just say that men require less time to use the bathroom, on average, than do women. It's simply faster when you don't have to sit down. Hence, longer lines for women.

It's often easier to treat people equally rather than fairly. Applying the concept of equal treatment to restrooms, for example, requires little thought. One makes a rule (five relief places for each sex) and applies it without much thought to differences that may be found in the audiences to which the rule is being applied. But is it fair if people are substantively different? If indeed the mechanics of going to the bathroom are to some degree substantively different for men than for women (which I am fairly certain they are), then we might expect a difference in the average time it takes for a woman to go and for a man to go. When a man says, as he departs to the bathroom, "I'll be back in a minute." That minute is more likely to be a literal 60 second minute. When a woman says it, there's a good chance that it's a figurative minute. I have to pause in my writing now to go relieve myself. I'll be back in a minute.

(Note: I've only been talking about the physical aspects of going to the bathroom. There are other differences. That's to say that while I have not done any scientific study, my informal observations suggest that women are more likely to use a bathroom trip as a mini social outing. Whereas I have observed women invite other women to the restroom, I have not personally witnessed this among men. That is, I have never heard one man say to another man, "Hey, come with me to the bathroom I need to talk to you about something." Not that this doesn't happen, I just have never personally observed it.)

The very fact that there is a difference in outcome among different groups produced by the application of an "equal treatment" of all groups" policy should trigger further inquiry and questioning. Note that I did not say that an equal treat ment policy is always wrong. What I implied is that it is not necessarily always correct in a world filled with myriad types of people representing multiple belief systems and ways of doing. If we live in a truly diverse world then "equal treat ment" approaches must always be examined under the microscope of fairness.

If my example of how real biological and sociological differences among men and women can impact going to the restroom did not convince you, consider this question. What are the possible outcomes of using standardized tests to evaluate students when students and the environments in which they live are un standard ized? Or how about this one? What if there is a policy to only promote people with good leadership attributes and qualities (not necessarily a bad policy) AND men (because they have historically held positions of leadership and got to write books on leadership) get to define what those qualities are (qualities often based on how they were raised and on male oriented societal expectations of what it means to be "a man")? Put differently, what could happen if a male-created mental model of how a leader should look and act looks and acts like a man? Might it contribute to the fact that, as of this writing, four hundred eighty nine (489) of the five hundred (500) Fortune 500 CEOs are men... in 2006? Oh yes, that's 97.8% of all the Fortune 500 CEOs. From a "glass half full" perspective that is a couple of percentage points better than it was several hundred years ago when 100% of the most powerful positions in the were held by men. Hurray for progress!

Fair as opposed to equal treatment entails more analysis and examination, maybe more research and consideration. It usually involves more time and more thinking. And it's likely to be a different type of thinking, requiring different thinkers with different perspectives around the table. If you are passionate about justice then give the concept of fairness a fair chance.

If you'll excuse me for a minute, I need to go visit the restroom again.

Our greatest glory is not in never falling, but in rising every time we fall.
~ Confucius ~

11
My Basketball Mentor

IN seventh grade I was 4 feet, 11 inches tall (or short) and really wanted to be on our junior high basketball team. I had adequate skills. My jump shot was sound, though more shot than jump, and my dribbling was excellent...if I only had to go right. I thought I had a chance.

Unfortunately, it seemed like every other person trying out for the team was at least a half-foot taller than me with "adequate" skills as well. So what do you think happened? Yep, I got cut. I was disappointed and angry, and out of frustration I even yelled at my mom for passing her short genes on to me, as if she had a choice and as if she had some tall genes to pass along to her progeny.

After sulking over the weekend, I arrived at school Monday morning to find a note left on my desk. The basketball coach wanted to talk with me after school.

I didn't know what to expect as I walked into his office. He gave me a big stack of papers and said, "Read this and do these things and you'll have a great chance of making the team next year."

I glanced through the papers. There were diagrams for plays and suggestions for exercises and drills Basically, it was a complete handbook for how to make a basketball team after you've been cut for being too short, too "right" and too slow. He said to me, "I'll help you if you want to listen and work hard. I'll show you what to do."

So I listened and worked hard. I did everything the coach suggested. The coach was great. I always felt he wanted me to succeed because he regularly talked to me and checked up on my progress. I worked out everyday (or at least

I like to remember it as every day), especially on building up my legs...getting stronger and quicker. I went from a 14 inch vertical jump to a 28 inch vertical jump in one year. I practiced dribbling with my left hand everyday (or at least I like to remember it as every day), and I sprouted to a towering 5 feet 2 inches!

Come eighth grade I was ready. And to make a long story short (pardon the pun), I not only made the team, I was the "sixth man" - the first player substituted from the bench. I was proud. My mother was proud. I think the coach was proud.

Looking back, I know I would not have made the team in eighth grade if the coach hadn't mentored me. If he hadn't given me that stack of papers, if he hadn't pushed me in the gym when I was tired, if he hadn't talked to me about strategy, then my chances for making the team would have been slim.

His help was crucial in my development as a young person, because the success that came from his guidance gave me much more confidence not only in sports, but also in social situations. It's unfortunate that it happens this way, but making the basketball team made others treat me with more respect. In fact, lots of positive things happened to me because my basketball coach cared enough to work with me, to share his secrets...to mentor me.

I still am not sure why he did it. Maybe it was because he knew I had the passion to be a basketball player, but no one to teach me how. Or maybe something about me reminded him of himself at a young age. Maybe he recognized that I really didn't have a dad that could teach me, like the other kids who made the team did (these kids had "built-in" mentors so to speak). Whatever it was, I still am glad to this day for his help, his advice and his tips. I'm thankful for his care.

Everyone has some knowledge base, some skill set, some special information that could help others, especially young people, taste success...to be successful. What personal assets do you have that you could share with someone else? You never know the positive impact you might have on another person, especially another young person, if you don't try. Let's try. Often that is the only difference between an intentional path maker and an unintentional path blocker. Which of these do you want to be remembered as?

We are apt to forget that children watch examples better than they listen to preaching.
~ Roy L. Smith ~

12
Do What They Say

IMAGINE having a young child who comes home from school. The two of you begin talking:

YOU: "How was your day today, honey?"
CHILD: "Okay."

YOU: "Just okay?"
CHILD: "Yep, just okay. (Pause) I was playing in class and wanted someone else to come play with me, so I asked Johnnie to come over to my station."

YOU: Did he come over, did he come and play with you?"
CHILD: "Nope, he gave me a funny look and said, 'I don't wanna play with you brownie!'"

YOU: (Concerned Pause) "Well...what did you do, honey?"
CHILD: "I looked right back at Johnnie and said, 'I don't think Martin Luther King would like you saying that!'"

Amazingly enough, this is a true story told to me by the mother of the CHILD. While she was proud of how her daughter responded, she also was saddened and concerned by what little "Johnnie" said. By the way, this short exchange took place in a kindergarten class...yes, 5 year olds.

This little case study teaches us at least two things. One, young children, even as young as five, are keenly able to learn bias and prejudice, as little John nie illustrates. But, the girl in our case study shows us that young children can learn the "right stuff" as well. The little girl knew when to invoke the concepts she was taught about Dr. Martin Luther King, Jr. Undoubtedly, she was taught those concepts intentionally with both words and behavioral reinforcement. Her parents modeled appropriate behavior for her.

Now let's take a look at Johnnie. Where might he have gone astray? It's likely that little Johnnie has very nice, sincere, kind and loving parents. They probably tell Johnnie, in little Johnnie words, to be nice and kind to everyone. They might even tell him not to judge people by their skin color, that everyone has value no matter what they look like.

But I'll bet that little Johnnie's parents never practice the behavior they preach. They probably never have people of color in their home. Little Johnnie probably rarely, if ever, sees his parents interact with people of color. Little Johnnie most likely never has had a babysitter of color.

Maybe the few times little Johnnie actually comes across people of color (other than a few at school) is when little Johnnie's parents take him to the "inner city" to volunteer at a soup kitchen...where he sees people of color who "fit the stereotype." This type of interaction often only reinforces the ideas little Johnnie already holds about people of color.

People, especially young ones, often learn behaviors by observing others. Ob viously, people also learn through verbal direction. But what happens when the verbal direction is in contrast with observable behavior? When there is dishar mony between the "talk" and the "walk," it often is the "walk" that gets picked-up.

Intentionally bringing the "talk" and the "walk" into balance on a consistent basis has the best chance of communicating desired attitudes and behaviors. This is true regardless of the age of the people you may be dealing with young or old or anywhere in between.

Doing what you say you believe becomes a matter of integrity, and thus trust. If parents tell their children that "diversity" is important, they should be prepared to back up their words with action. If not, then they should not be surprised when their little Johnnies end up sounding like our little Johnnie in the story. Likewise, when organizations say they value everyone and celebrate diversity, they ought to have concrete behavioral evidence to support it. Not living up to and acting out stated values is a quick way to engender distrust.

Unfortunately, little Johnnie picked up some misconceptions in his short five years. The question is, "Will he unlearn them so that he can effectively and suc cessfully exist in the diverse world that awaits him?" Hopefully, his parents have recognized this teachable moment and are preparing him by talking about and modeling appropriate behavior. Or, simply, by doing what they say.

The eye sees only what the mind is prepared to comprehend.
~ Henri Bergson ~

13
It's in the Details

WHEN my oldest son was just 18 months old he had two canine encounters that affect him to this day. The first came on a nice spring day while he was playing in our backyard. As he was playing with his assortment of toy cars and trucks, the neighbor's dog came running over, and before I could react, the little dog "lovingly attacked" my son, licking his face, jumping on him and knocking him down. That's something that excited, playful dogs do, and this dog meant no harm. As you can imagine my son was quickly in tears.

Shortly after that incident, my son encountered a much bigger dog at a local park. In the midst of eating some pizza during our picnic, a good sized German shepherd wandered in from nearby and attempted to snatch my son's piece of pizza from his hands. At first my son held on tight unwilling to give up his lunch. The dog, as stubborn, let my son know who the eventual winner would be by producing a menacing growl. My son quickly let go and in the process fell down hurting his behind. Again, the tears flowed.

Whether it was the incident in the park or the combination of the two tear filled encounters I do not know, but from that point forth my son was deathly afraid of ALL dogs. Even as an 11 year old, my son is still deathly afraid of dogs. Doesn't matter their size. Doesn't matter their demeanor. Doesn't matter what they are doing. In my son's mind, dogs are something to be feared. A dog could be the nicest canine in the world, but my son will not go near it.

An interesting thing is that my oldest son can watch his three younger siblings play with a dog, and still he won't approach it. He can see that the dog isn't harming his brothers and sister, but that isn't proof that the dog will be equally harmless to him. I thought he would "outgrow" the incident he had as a toddler, but his fear today is as strong as it was then.

On one level, I can't understand my son's fear of every dog he sees, especially when there is observable evidence that a particular dog is not dangerous. On a different level my inability to understand is clear. The problem I have in understanding my son's "irrational" fear is that I try to understand it from my perspective. It's easy for me not to be afraid of dogs since I've never had a bad encounter with a dog. I know that some dogs can be mean and dangerous. I also know that many are playful and harmless. The reality in which I dwell leads me to examine clues that might distinguish a potentially threatening dog from a playful one. My son's reality does not include that type of examination.

A major problem that many of us have in understanding the actions of others is that we often evaluate their actions against the backdrop of what we would do in the same situation. That attempt to walk in another's shoes in itself is not necessarily problematic. The problem arises when the shoes we are walking in are believed to be their shoes when they are actually our own. Put another way, when we make attributions and judgments about the behaviors of others based on our own limited experiences and knowledge of "others" we are likely to make mistakes. Why? Because we fill in the gaps of knowledge we have with information that comes straight out of our own reality, our own world, our own belief system. This is what I have labeled and refer to as being "empa centric (as opposed to empathetic).

Empathy and being empathetic have to do with being able to identify with another's thoughts, feelings, and attitudes. Being genuinely empathetic requires, to a great degree, knowledge about the other, their history, their reality, their world. Without adequate knowledge we are to some degree guessing at what it would be like—and we are apt to be more or less "empa-centric." The empa-centric person, who may sincerely desire to be empathetic, brings along all their assets in answering the question, "What would I do in their shoes?"

We saw a prime example of this following Hurricane Katrina in 2005. I'm sure you heard or read accounts of people, who were no where close to New Orleans, say things like, "If I knew the hurricane was coming days in advance, I would have got out of there." These folks in their empa-centrism and inability to truly identify with what it might be like for those in New Orleans at the time incorporated their reality into the decision making algorithm. I'm sure some were imagining themselves, with knowledge of the hurricane in advance, driving out of New Orleans in their new Lexus!

If you didn't hear those types of comments after Katrina, there is no doubt that you've been privy to conversations in which some has said, "I'd never act like that..." or "What would possess someone to do something like that?" When we mentally re create the situation to evaluate our own response, we sometimes leave out important "details" (sometimes intentionally and some unintention ally) that likely would impact how we would truly act given the exact same circumstances. We tend to be empa centric when trying to walk in the shoe of others, especially of others who are very different than our selves. Heck, many times we can't even get out of our own shoes!

No wonder it's hard for many white folks to understand and accept it when people of color bring up race as a recurring issue. If one never experiences what it's like being "non-white" in a white-dominated workforce and/or doesn't know much about the country's racialized history, then it's easy to dismiss affirmative action policies as unfair and unneeded, and to make accusations of using the "race card."

If someone isn't gay or has no gay or lesbian friends, then it often is difficult to accept that homosexuality may actually not be a choice or how painful it can be to live out one's life in a culture and world designed for heterosexuals.

If someone is not a woman, then it is harder to believe that those "harmless" jokes told in the workplace contribute to a "glass ceiling" in many organiza tions.

If someone is part of the dominant culture and benefits from the status quo, then it is easier to label attempts to produce greater fairness, justice and equity as acts of "political correctness."

If I tried to understand my son's fear of dogs without taking into consider ation his two encounters with our neighbor's dog and the dog in the park, then I would call his fear irrational, baseless, and incomprehensible. But by taking those "details" into account, I have a greater appreciation and understanding of why he clings to my leg when a dog approaches.

By validating his fear as rational and understandable, I give myself patience to figure out creative approaches and, ultimately, solutions for reducing his fear of dogs. More importantly though, when I validate his fear, I validate him as a person, as a human being that deserves respect and understanding.

So the next time you catch yourself saying or thinking something like, "It's nothing, quit being so sensitive," or "Why do you have to see it that way?" ask yourself if you've taken enough "details" into account. Oh yes, and ask yourself if those types of comments and questions come from an empathetic heart or an "empa-centric" one. The former cares. The latter blames.

Culture is the acquired knowledge people use to interpret experience
and generate behavior.
~ James Spradley ~

14
Below the Surface

MY brother recently called me to start planning our annual Canadian fishing trip. It's a big family event that all five brothers eagerly await. Avid fishermen, we take the sport seriously, or at least as seriously as we can without people call ing us obsessive. Those "people" are our wives who find our attachment to rods, reels and Rapalas just a little unnatural.

While our trip to the "Great White North" usually involves a hunt for Walleye and Pike, I've been pushing for a place to pull out my fly rod for some trout. Fly-fishing is something I got into a few years back.

I don't remember exactly how fly-fishing first caught my fancy, but for some reason the movie "A River Runs Through It" strikes a chord. Critics gave the movie a "thumbs up" for its theme, story line and lessons. I liked all those scenes of big trout being caught on bamboo fly rods. It was a glimpse of heaven to me, watching those boys whip figure eights with their fly-lines and cast their bug-like bait with pinpoint accuracy. But what most intrigued me was watching the fly drift lazily on top of the current then, without warning, get interrupted by a mighty splash. Now that's fly-fishing. Or so I thought.

After watching the movie, I went to buy fly-fishing equipment at a local fly-fishing shop. When I first walked into the store, I looked around in amazement at all the equipment, enough to plunge the purchaser into poverty. As I loitered in a mix of confusion and awe, the storeowner, an elderly gentlemen, broke me out of my trance, "Somethin' I can help you with?" I told him I had just seen "A

River Runs Through It" and wanted to get into fly-fishing. He gave a little laugh and queried further, "Do you want to really learn how to fly-fish or do you want to do it the way you saw in the movie?

I was stumped. I didn't know there was a difference. He began to explain, "What you saw in the movie is not how real fly-fishers fish."

"Real fly-fishers?" I mumbled.

"Yes, real fly-fishers are the ones who actually catch big fish on a consistent basis. They don't do that movie stuff."

"What do you mean that movie stuff?"

He continued, "In the movie all you saw were people fishing with what we call dry flies, flies that float on top of the water."

I interrupted, "Yea, isn't that fly-fishing, casting a fly, letting it float down stream and waiting for a fish to come up and get it?"

"That's only a small part of fly-fishing. When you're fishing for trout, you have to understand that 90% of the time trout, especially the big ones, eat un der the surface of the water. For example, trout generally grab nymphs as the nymphs are making their way to the surface   they rarely break the surface to eat. Most of the action takes place where you can't see it. It's easy to think that fly-fishing is what they portrayed in the movie, but in reality, the best fly-fishers use what we call wet flies and nymphs that don't float. To be an effective fly-fisher you have to be keenly aware of what happens below the surface of the water."

As he finished his coaching session, I began to understand that what I be lieved to be the entirety of fly-fishing was only the small, "showy" part of this wonderful sport. Perhaps most people who don't know much about fly-fishing think about it the way I did   surface action, easily seen.

I suppose it is very much the same way with issues of discrimination, whether it 's racism, sexism, ageism, homophobia, etc. Those who have not faced or witnessed much discrimination tend only to recognize it in obvious acts   that "surface action" easily recognized by most people.

Those acts include cross burnings or crude, demeaning jokes directed at women in the workplace, for example, or words like "faggot" and "queer" writ ten on the walls and mirrors of offices. This is obvious discrimination, the "dry flies" of prejudice and exclusion. But, these acts make up only a small percent age of all discriminatory behavior.

It's the remaining 90% of discrimination that should catch most of our at tention. It's the "under the surface," subtle activities that cause the most harm. Unfortunately, a majority of us can't, don't or won't look below the surface to see what's happening. And often, when we are told what's happening below the surface, our reaction tends to be one of disbelief or amazement.

Most discriminatory behaviors, even our own acts, occur beneath the thresh old of our daily awareness. Often, we see and don't recognize. For those of us who fall into that category (I dare say that's all of us), our job is to put on the wet gear and dive below the surface to experience, engage and encounter lives that have been, for the most part, below our level of awareness.

In doing so, we might begin to see a whole new world. It is a world that might shock and frighten us at first, but one that we will come to understand. And with understanding will come less fear, more comfort and greater appreciation for all those things that make us unique   and all those things that we have in common. Strangers will become less strange.

Where do you spend the majority of your time addressing issues of discrimination, inequality and injustice? Is it with "surface action" issues that are easily seen, but may not get at the root of the matter, or is it with the tougher, less obvious issues that aren't as splashy but offer greater rewards?

The measure of a wise person is the ability to entertain new ideas without nec essarily having to accept them.
~ Aristotle ~

15
I Know Everything Already

"YOU don't know what you don't know." I'm sure you've heard that saying before. It certainly makes sense that you can't know that of which you have no knowledge. The problem is that many of us, including myself, think we know more than we actually do. Or, worse, we believe that the limited knowledge we have about something is comprehensive, and moreover, that it's absolutely true. When challenged, we resist the notion that we could be wrong. "It can't be that way," we say to ourselves, "that's not what I learned."

Well, if you would allow me to embarrass myself a little, you might find a les son about the need to emphasize our curiosity about the world and other people while minimizing some of the certainty about things we think we know. It's also a story about how ignorance and arrogance make a formidable duo that prevents us from exploring new perspectives and ideas.

It was several years ago that I was teaching a freshmen level class on critical inquiry and expression. Among other things, the course required students to ex plore their world with a critical eye focused through a lens of multiculturalism.

One of the first assignments was for students to write a short paper about an experience that taught them something significant. There was great variety in the quality of the finished products, with many of the papers well written and oth ers...well, let's just say that I ran out of ink marking them up.

Several of the students' stories still are fresh in my memory, and not necessar ily because they were terrific, but because they illustrated some of the ways that first-year students' brains are hard-wired. The paper that taught me the most was written by a young woman, and I don't even remember exactly what she wrote about. But it involved cheerleading and those things that become an extension of every cheerleader's hands   you know, Pom Poms.

Again, I don't remember much about her paper except that I wrote a lot on it. I do remember that the four pages consisted of only three paragraphs, and that she didn't know the meaning of the word "literally." She wrote that she "had literally died when she got off the bus," which means she must have been literally resur rected to come to my class. But that's not what struck me most. No, it was all the times I had to circle spelling errors, mainly the misspelling of "Pom Poms," which she spelled with an "n," as in "Pom Pons." Her paper played a major role in reducing the ink in my pen. But since it was her first paper, I gave her a grade based more on effort than ability.

Shortly after I returned the papers back to the class, the woman who wrote the "cheerleading" paper approached me with a question. She pointed to all the times I circled "Pom Pons" on her paper and asked, "What's wrong with that?" I told her that the word is misspelled, and she countered that that "Pom Pons" actually is the correct spelling.

"How dare she argue with me," I thought. Doesn't this little brat know that the three letters behind my name, Ph.D., make me an expert—about everything, including the spelling of Pom Poms? Obviously, she could care less about the Ph.D. that I worked so hard to get. I could have had M.A., B.A., ESPN, NBC, CNN, SBC, AAA or NBA behind my name. To her, the letters might make me an "expert" in some areas, but not in cheerleading. She probably was thinking there should be a four letter word behind my name.

As she continued to protest, I dug in deeper. My "Pom Pom" fortress would not crumble. It would not crack, especially under pressure from this bothersome freshman gnat. Didn't she know that I won my district's spelling bee in third grade? The harder she pushed, the more certain I became about my position. It is "Pom Poms!"

As I tried to shoo her away, she reached into her book bag to pull something out. Thoughts flashed in my head about psycho students who shoot their profes sors over a poor grade. Could this be happening? After fumbling in her bag for what seemed like minutes, she drew her weapon. I flinched as she turned back toward me. "Here's a dictionary. Look it up if you don't believe me."

With great confidence, I took the dictionary and began paging through it, all the while picturing her forthcoming apology for even questioning my cheerlead ing equipment acumen. "There," I said, "it's Pom Poms."

She looked at me with surprise, "Are you sure?"

Just to appease her, I put my finger on the word and said, "See for yourself."

She looked closer at the dictionary, then eyed me with disgust. "According to this dictionary, it's spelled Pom Pons." I looked again. She was right. It was spelled with an "n."   How did I miss it? Though the evidence was right before my eyes, I didn't want to believe it. "Must be a mistake," I thought to myself. "How could I have learned it incorrectly? Did she publish her own dic tionary in her quest for a better grade? How could I be wrong? I have a Ph.D." All these questions ran through my mind. Although I still wasn't convinced 100 percent, I told her I would reassess her paper. And after leaving the classroom, I went back to my office to check my dictionary. It too had the wrong spelling. "It can't be," I thought. All my life I have been told its "Pom Poms."

My certainty was shaken by this young whippersnapper who basically told me, "Hey stupid, the world is round, not flat!" In the end, I had to admit that I was wrong. The world is indeed round.   In wondering about how I could have been wrong all those years, I realized that there was never a time in my life when I heard someone say "Pom Pons." I always have heard it pronounced "Pom Poms." Maybe people have said "Pom Pons" to me, but I filtered it into "Pom Poms." People who "taught" me learned it incorrectly, and passed their mistake to me. Moreover, I don't recall ever seeing the term written anywhere, until encountering it in this student's paper.

When it comes to people, is it possible that we hold information that we be lieve to be true when in fact it's greatly distorted. Could it be that we live shel tered from people different than ourselves, which has led us to believe "Pom Poms" about others when in fact the reality is "Pom Pons?"

The natural thing to do when our "world" is being challenged is to defend our turf. On gender issues, I've heard more than once, "We don't have any women in leadership positions, but we aren't sexist." Then, when challenged further, we come up with great rationalizations for our position. "Women just haven't been in the workplace as long as men," as if every man in leadership has worked a long time to achieve that position. It couldn't be true that males have devel oped a structure and network that, for the most part, hinders the advancement of women. We tell women that they just need to work harder. Or we tell them not to have kids, or that they are too emotional and read too much into things. Nope, it couldn't be that the "real" world is a little different than the tidy little world we have in our mind. After all, it's "Pom Poms," right?

That incident taught me that some parts, potentially many parts of my knowl edge base may have faulty data, that I may have been given bad information throughout my life. That realization is tough to accept because it forces me to question much of the information I have about my world. I have to start asking myself, "Where did I learn that? Was the source credible? Have I been exposed to different perspectives? Am I too arrogant to admit that I could be wrong, or that I am wrong? Am I willing to step out of my comfort zone to grow?" In an age of technology where we have access to many types of information from myriad sources, many of us still gravitate to what is familiar, what "speaks our language" and doesn't challenge us much. And therein lies the trap. Our quest for comfort and stability leaves us defensive in the face of new and different ideas.

So how will you and your organization react when the "new" and the "differ ent" are no longer easily ignored? Will you open up to other possibilities, though they may initially cause embarrassment or even pain? Or will you be like 15th and 16th century leaders who stood by their position even after many had evi dence that the Earth revolves around the sun, not the other way around.

My challenge to those of us who tend to be certain about our world is this: Minimize certainty and maximize curiosity, especially when it comes to people and ideas with which we have very little interaction. There is much to learn from being more curious.

By the way, are you supposed to capitalize "Pom Pons?"

What you see and hear depends a good deal on where you are standing; it also depends on what sort of person you are.
~ C.S. Lewis ~

16
Someday They Will See

IMAGINE living in a community where a small percentage of the population upholds the Christian faith. You are "one of those Christians." Your forefathers founded this community many generations ago, but over the course of time non Christians "took over" and became the majority.

Many years ago the non Christians started a school, and to honor those who first settled the community they decided to have as their mascot, the "Christians." Now, they never consulted Christians in the community about naming the mas cot. They didn't even talk with anyone about how best to honor the community's founding fathers.

These non Christians didn't know much about the Christian faith except that Christians, they noticed, hold something called Communion on a regular basis. The non Christians observed this Communion process, eating bread and drink ing wine, and saw that nearly all Christians participate.

They decided that since "Christians" is the school's mascot, they should have it do something Christian like at school assemblies and athletic competitions. The non Christians saw this as a way to build school and community pride, so they chose this "Communion" thing as the perfect ritual to perform at school functions. Not only would it generate pride, they reasoned, but it also will show that non Christians value the Christians in the community.

As you hear about the plan, you quickly suggest to the non Christians that what they are going to do would not honor the Christian faith, but actually dis honor it. You tell them that taking Communion is a sacred act of meaningful significance to Christians and that, in fact, taking Communion for fun and show is blasphemous to many Christians.

As you make your objections, many non Christians become defensive. In fact, they take offense at your objections and insist that you should be thankful for their efforts in bringing attention to a wonderful Christian ritual. You repeat your objections over and over, but the more you protest, the more they dig in their heels. Indeed, the more you object, the more they believe what they are doing is an honoring gesture. They vehemently argue that they have good inten tions and that you are taking this "Communion thing" way too seriously. They tell you to lighten up.

By this time, the re enactment of Communion has become a regular part of half time activities at basketball and football games. People in the stands create motions around it, putting their hands to their mouth twice once to signify the eating of the bread and once to show the drinking of wine when their team needs support. They've even added a life sized cross with a real student tied to it for "effect." Non-Christians in the community love it. They identify with it. They are full of school and community pride when they see it.

You and others in the Christian community continue to object. But since you are thought of as the "minority," no one listens. Community and school lead ers tell you to "Get over it!" They continue their insistence that there's nothing wrong with what they are doing, and that they won't be bullied by "political cor rectness."

The heart of the Christian community sinks. Your defense of a significant act of faith has been deemed an act of political correctness. Though what they do inflicts pain on you and other Christians, you know that the non-Christians don't know what they are doing. You forgive them in the midst of your pain, suffering and humiliation. You go on. You learn to survive. You say to yourself and other Christians, "Someday they will see."

How much do you know about American Indians and their approach to spiri tuality and worship? If you don't know much, you might consider doing a little study. Maybe then you might see why the "mascot thing" is a big deal to many American Indians. Maybe you'll begin to understand that the issues go well beyond hurtful stereotypes. You might even begin to empathize with the argu ment that allowing a team in our national's capitol to have an American Indian mascot, at the least, borders on institutionalized racial prejudice (read: Racism). That simple "mascot thing" turns out to be much more complex than many real ize.

When we know little about others, what they believe and value, we shouldn't be surprised when we make mistakes in our cross cultural interactions, and yet we often are. Then, amazingly enough as we stand like the proverbial deer in headlights, we often find ways to blame others, distancing ourselves from re sponsibility and relieving ourselves of culpability. How so? We tell others that they are being "too sensitive." We accuse them of playing the "race card." In our righteousness we recommend that they "pull themselves up by their boot straps." In our arrogance we hold firm that the "playing field is level." Does any of this sound familiar?

A wise person once offered me some profound words, telling me that, "Life is a game of error-correction." But more profound were the challenging words that followed, "Are you humble enough to admit your mistakes and courageous enough to correct them?" Effectively engaging "diversity" and walking in the worlds of others requires well meaning, compassionate and fair minded people to live mindfully, embrace humility and act courageously. Are you up to the task, or is just easier to believe that "those Indians" are making much too big a deal out of that mascot thing?

If you are leaping a ravine, the moment of takeoff is a bad time to be consider
ing alternative strategies.
~ John Cleese ~

17
Expectation Violations

ONCE upon a time in a place not so far away there was a company called WECAN. This company was known for its WECAN soft drink, a refreshing fruit drink that truly was a unique product in the market. While WECAN's drink did not have mass appeal, it did attract a loyal group of fruit drink enthusiasts. This group was large enough and had enough buying power to make WECAN a very successful company.

Because WECAN's base of customers was so loyal, the company never marketed its drink. Executives believed that they could rely forever on the devotion of their customers and on word of mouth. But times changed. WECAN's competitors were able to duplicate the fruit drink. Competitors poured millions of dollars into advertising and targeted a broader customer base, so they found many others who enjoyed the drink. They even converted some of WECAN's loyal followers to their drink.

WECAN became alarmed, and company executives decided they must do something   quickly. They agreed to begin marketing their drink...in a big way. Marketing became a core strategy, a core value, a business imperative. They believed everything the company did had to be done through a marketing lens, and with full support from the top, WECAN began addressing its marketing problem.

Because of its early success, which included little marketing (and no marketing strategy), WECAN did not have a marketing department, a marketing team or anyone with marketing expertise. WECAN knew it had to put a marketing team together. It was suggested that someone with marketing expertise and experience should be brought in to help this new marketing team, but that idea quickly was brushed aside. WECAN executives felt they easily could put together a team comprised of existing employees. Since all the employees were consumers themselves and had experience at the other end of marketing, WECAN leadership reasoned that they had the skills to devise a great marketing strategy.

The marketing team had a diverse membership representing many areas of the company and many consumer perspectives. Some members were selected because the WECAN fruit drink was not their favorite. Others were chosen because they read a lot of magazines and could give the "print media" perspective. Still others were picked because they buy many products off the Internet and could give the "online" perspective. Finally, others were brought on board because they had taken a marketing class in college. Everyone on the team was passionate about developing a strategic marketing plan that would increase WECAN's share of the market and ensure its future success.

The team met for many months and came up with various ideas. Some were implemented and failed. Others showed initial success, but quickly became ineffective. Still more were developed, but never executed. Members of the marketing team became frustrated and disillusioned. They felt they had done so many good things. They were confident their ideas were good, especially in light of the fact that no one on the team had any expertise or training in marketing.

Eventually, the marketing team was just going through the motions. Many lost their passion. Others "knew" this would happen. They couldn't understand why their "great" ideas were not working.

Finally, because of its failure to develop a sound, strategic and informed marketing strategy, WECAN was overtaken by competitors in its niche market. Fortunately, WECAN had enough loyal customers to survive, but everyone at WECAN knew that they had let a great opportunity slip away. They would not become the big success that they had envisioned.

Does this in any way describe the way your organization goes about addressing diversity and inclusion? Do you put together a diversity team or council in the manner the WECAN Company put together its marketing team? Does your diversity team represent diversity, but include no one who actually has any experience and skills in developing strategies and activities around diversity and inclusion?

I have observed numerous organizations with great passion and intentions make this fundamental error. Just because someone is of color, gay, disabled, female, etc., does not necessarily mean they have experience or expertise in developing a strategic diversity and inclusion plan. They may have experience in telling you "how it is," but be of little assistance in helping you change "how it is."

If diversity and inclusion is a core belief deemed vitally important to the success of your organization, then what are you doing to show that it is that significant? It's a good thing to have a "diversity and inclusion team" and, hopefully the team is diverse. But if this group is charged with developing inclusive strategies designed to positively impact the entire organization, then look strongly at developing an appropriate level of expertise within the team.

Ideally you would have a senior level executive with substantial experience in the area of diversity & inclusion. But whether it's a "Senior VP of Diversity & Inclusion" or an external consultant, getting expert help when you have very little (or none) is crucial. Getting the necessary assistance to jumpstart your diversity and inclusion efforts helps to ensure you are doing diversity right (read: as a strategic business imperative), instead of just doing diversity (read: as a "flavor of the month.")

Put it this way: Is the marketing department, finance department, IT department or any "vital" department in your organization comprised of people with little or no experience in those respective areas? I thought not.

The beginning is the most important part of any work.
~ Plato ~

18
What If?

RECENTLY, a small but growing community was challenged with a pro posal to build a rather large shopping mall. Community planners had conducted studies that suggested the community was in need of a shopping mall, and that a mall would benefit the community's economy. The studies showed that there were enough people to support a mall and that many in the community desired a shopping center. Those in favor mainly cited the convenience of having a nearby mall.

To further gather people's input, there was a series of community meetings to discuss the proposed mall. Many who attended the meetings expressed delight at the prospect of having a mall in their community. Many said the community was growing significantly and that it was about time to get its own mall. Overall, the concept of a new mall was well received.

Then the question was asked, "Where exactly will this mall be located?" Ac cording to the planners, the best site for the mall was a location relatively close to a residential neighborhood. The site was optimal for a host of reasons includ ing traffic and available land. Once the proposed site was disclosed, many who initially favored the development of a mall balked. Not unexpectedly, people closest to the proposed site were most vocal in their opposition.

Many residents who became concerned after finding out where the mall would be built still wanted to have a mall. They still believed the community needed a mall, and they still wanted convenient access to a mall. They even said that a new mall would make a significant, positive economic impact on the community. They just didn't want to have the mall near their homes.

The community meetings dragged on and on as those who opposed the mall asked more and more questions and raised more and more concerns. The plan ners warned the community that if it did not grant permission to proceed soon, a nearby community would take advantage of the opportunity.

Several months passed. The community remained undecided. Those who still opposed the mall conceded that it would have a positive impact. They knew that the mall would attract significant numbers of people - and money - from the sur rounding areas. They even understood that the public tax revenue would be used to improve the schools, community services and other things that benefit the entire community. They still opposed.

Eventually, the mall developer told the community that she could wait no lon ger. While the community debated, she received approval from a nearby com munity. Groundbreaking would get underway in the "other" community in a few months.

Years passed. The community that built the mall showed strong, dynamic growth. It was able to use revenue from the mall to enhance public services. The mall attracted other businesses that grew the tax base even more. Basically, the community had been reborn and its future looked bright.

Meanwhile, the community that "lost out" on the mall was stagnant. It de creased in population. Tax revenues dropped as businesses left, many relocating to the nearby community that had built the mall. The outlook for this community was not as positive. Many were asking, "What if?"

Which of the above communities is your organization? How is your orga nization addressing the changing reality of our world? Will you wax and wane in the face of strong, significant evidence that you take diversity and inclusion seriously? Will your indecision put you behind competitors who understand and believe the competitive advantage found in diversity? Is your organization the type that truly values diversity and inclusion?

Many organizations will claim positive attitudes toward diversity...until "di versity" hits close to home. Many conceptually understand the benefits of di versity and inclusion, but find reasons not to pursue them. It's kind of like the community members that wanted the mall, but did not want it next to them. That community eventually lost out to a "competitor" community that took seriously the data and acted with conviction.

Again, which of the above communities is your organization? Don't be the one asking "What if?" after the fact. Companies that do so often find themselves asking "What now?" as their competitors pass them by.

You're more likely to act yourself into feeling than feel yourself into action.
~ Jerome Bruner ~

19
I Hate Board Games

THERE I was minding my own business at another family get together, dinner nicely settling in my "tummy," giving me that glazed-over, sleepy feeling. Just this side of blissful rapid eye movement, almost oblivious to the television showing another Detroit Lions loss, I hear the dreaded words, "Let's play board games!"

These are not normal, everyday words to me. They elicit a guttural response from which humankind has been trying to escape for thousands of years. I can't bear to hear them. I fear my "Mr. Hyde" will show himself. "Stop!" I scream within the confines of my mind. But again they attack, "Anyone wanna play board games?"

I feign sleeping, hopeful that they find enough players without requiring my participation. On this occasion, I want to be the poor kid who gets picked last... or not at all. I hear people stirring around me as they make their way to another room. "Yes!" I dare not peak at what's going on, but it sounds like the coast is clear. The old spiritual tune rings in my head, "Free at last, free at last, thank God almighty I'm free at last."

Then I feel a tap on my arm. I do not react. Then, I feel another tap. "Leave me alone!" I want to say. But instead, the words that strike the air are these: "Wake up Uncle Steve, we're going to play Monopoly!" The gig is up. I surrender. My eyes open to my little nephew smiling at me: "Let's go, Uncle Steve!" Whose kid is this anyway? "C'mon, they're starting Uncle Steve." He is relentless. All I can think of is the "Borg" species from the Star Trek: Next Generation series, aliens that assimilate all living beings into their "hive." Resistance is futile, so I get out of the Lazy Boy and slump off to prison...err, the game table. The Monopoly board is prepared.

To make matters worse, I'm the Thimble. I can't be the Race Car or the Shoe, I have to be the Thimble. I've got a bad attitude before the game even begins. I see no way that the situation can improve. But something strange happens along the way. People are talking and laughing. My nephew tells a joke   a bad joke, but people laugh. I catch myself laughing.

"Okay, this is not so bad," I think. I am enjoying the game. Heck, I'm taking people's money, too! By the end of the game, my attitude about board games has changed completely. Well, maybe not completely, but I'm on my way to becom ing a board game advocate...so long as I'm not the Thimble.

Many times in our lives, we have bad attitudes about things we are asked to do. We don't want to do them, but in the midst of the process, we often discover that it's not that bad. Sometimes, like me, we even find that we enjoy ourselves and walk away with a "new" attitude.

I often am asked if I think diversity training should be required or voluntary. My question in return is, "How important is inclusion to your organization?" Does it make sense to value all of your human resources? Does it make your organization better and more competitive when your workforce embraces and values diversity and inclusion in an increasingly global society?

If you "require" training and education in other areas of your organization why do you do so? Likely it's because the skills that are obtained through the training benefit your organization. Why is it any different with respect to train ing and education around diversity and inclusion? If diversity and inclusion is a core value for your organization, if you believe that it's a good thing to have all employees feel valued and included (i.e., engaged) the answer to questions about diversity training is pretty clear.

Many organizations don't want to mandate "diversity training" because they believe people have a bad attitude about it   that it will just make things worse. So diversity training becomes voluntary...and the "choir" hears more preaching. Many people have negative mindsets about diversity training, but the problem is not with the concept, it's the way the training takes place. It's the way the leader ship prepares the organization for that type of training. Diversity training must be framed within the context of continuous organizational improvement. It must be "sold" as a benefit to everyone. This starts with leadership and flows to every part of the organization.

People's bad attitudes toward diversity training likely will change when they see how it benefits them and the organization as a whole. Contrary to conven tional wisdom, behavior does not always stem from attitude. Sometimes, behav ior can have a powerful impact on changing someone's attitude. Negative atti tudes about diversity training can be changed, if the training is done well. Who knows? Maybe those who once viewed "diversity" like I viewed board games will find that board games can be fun... and a strategic advantage, too!

Hopefully your organization is providing "diversity and inclusion" training and education, and framing it in such a way that your people see it as vital to the organization. If the leaders of your organization are not communicating to your folks that such training is about organizational development, about total em ployee engagement, about creativity and innovation, about continuous improve ment, then don't be surprised to hear all the negative rumblings about "diversity training."

The soul, like the body, accepts by practice whatever
habit one wishes it to contact.
~ Socrates ~

20
Use One More Club

IT'S late February and there's a half foot of snow on the ground, but I am thinking golf. Why not? The pro golf tour started weeks ago, teasing me every weekend as if to say, "Hey you, sitting in your winter wonderland, watch us play golf in lush Hawaii, warm Florida and sunny California. And by the way, we're making truckloads of money hitting a little white ball, and you're not."

If you're a golfer stuck in a wintery state like Michigan, you have the bug by now. And if you have the bug, you are a "real golfer." (Note that I did not say "good golfer." Being a "real golfer" and being a "good golfer" can be mutually exclusive things.) We real golfers are an odd bunch, itching to spend hundreds, even thousands of dollars every golf season so we might improve our game by one or two strokes. Our hard earned money gets sucked into a big black hole so we can tell others how well we sunk a little ball into a little black hole. We dream of telling people we knocked a 200-yard 4-iron stiff, within two feet of the flag, and tend to leave out the part about three putting the remaining two footer.

For me, and I suspect many other golfers, every season begins the same. We have glorious visions of consistently driving 250+ yards...and straight. We see ourselves hitting 8 irons 165 yards, though past history suggests otherwise. Our thoughts are filled with draining 15-foot putts, memories of missed two-footers

purged by the cleansing snow   or maybe by playing with people who offer gen
erous "gimmes."

This year, for my "be a better golfer project," I have written the words "take
one more club." When practicing, I can hit my 8-iron as far as 160 yards...okay,
150 yards. For some reason, I believe I can hit that distance with my 8 iron
when I play on the course. Many golfers, like myself, are an overly optimistic,
"I am much better than I really am" group of people. We believe that if we can
do something in practice three out of ten times, then we certainly should be able
to do it on the course nine out of ten times. And we get angry when it doesn't
happen that way. We have really good attitudes about great execution, but our
positive attitudes rarely translate to the desired outcome.

The golfer's mentality is much like the duality suggested by Greek philoso
pher Socrates, that there exist primarily two worlds   the perfect and the imper
fect. In the perfect world, I routinely hit my 8 iron 160 yards...okay, 150. Able
to execute perfectly every time, I don't have to worry about sand traps, the long
grass in back of the green or the water in front. These obstacles do not come into
play in my perfect world because my shots are perfect.

In my imperfect world, however, those obstacles are real. In that world, mis
placed divots are my trademark. Big ones, little ones, thick ones and thin ones...
it's not unusual for chunks of earth and grass to fly farther than my ball. I am
targeted by golf course maintenance crews for extinction in my imperfect world,
where 8-irons erratically fly only 140 yards.

The duality of perfect and imperfect worlds extends beyond golf. We think
that we do things and behave exceedingly well in other areas of life, too. "Of
course I'm not biased. No way do I have prejudice. I treat everyone the same. I
only judge on ability." These are words found in the perfect world. And some
how, they've made their way to the imperfect world, the real world.

When it comes to diversity and inclusion, we all have a tendency to think
of ourselves as "relatively perfect." Sure, we make mistakes, but they are few.
Seeing ourselves in an overly positive, optimistic light can blind us to the im
perfections in our daily interactions. In our perfect world, many of us embrace
and value the concept of diversity. So we find it difficult to accept the notion
that we don't "do diversity" well. Realistically we should not be surprised when
we make mistakes, since many of us rarely practice "diversity" in our everyday
interactions. In that way, diversity is much like golf.

We golfers expect to play well even if we don't practice, which for most golf
ers means slapping balls on the range for five minutes before tee time (isn't that
enough?). We then wonder why, in the heat of competition with 25 cents on the
line, we buckle under the pressure of a two foot putt.

How many of us give ourselves the opportunity to "practice" interacting with
others unlike ourselves? Or do we just expect to execute correctly when the
time arises? Face it, unless we prepare and practice for the changing realities
of our world, we shouldn't be shocked when our attempts at "doing diversity"

fall short. Just as it is hard to hit a golf ball accurately and consistently when we don't practice, it's difficult to be good at diversity and inclusion when we don't engage "diversity" consistently and practice "inclusion" accurately.

Living out diversity and inclusion, like life, is a journey of error correction. And if such is the case, the question for all of us becomes, "Are we willing to admit our mistakes, and courageous enough to correct them?"

No, not try. Do or do not. There is no try.
~ Yoda ~

21
The Kingdom of Athemba

ONCE upon a time in the kingdom of Athemba, there flowed a magical river. The Mighty River's water, pure and clear and bubbling with vigor, had a super natural quality that was the source of life to the kingdom. Flowing swiftly from one end of the kingdom to the other, the river was the foundation on which Ath emba was built and prospered. Without the Mighty River, life in Athemba would have been difficult.

Because of its magical powers, the people of Athemba settled as close as pos sible to the Mighty River, lining it with numerous homes, buildings and shops. The banks of the river bustled, and the citizens of Athemba became quite com fortable with the carefree, easy living the river enabled. Their lifestyles took the Mighty River for granted...but change was peaking over the horizon.

In this time, a great queen named Zawa ruled the Kingdom of Athemba. She was a wise leader, who was loved and respected by all in the kingdom. Known as a woman of great integrity, Zawa always did what she said she would do. She understood that the life of the kingdom and its citizens flowed with the currents of the Mighty River, and she did much to protect it.

For the past few years, Queen Zawa's trusted scientists had been noticing a drop in the water level of the Mighty River. At first they thought nothing of it, expecting a return to normal in following years, as the river had done in the past. But the growing evidence suggested that "normal" would never return, and this worried the scientists. They requested a meeting with Queen Zawa and her lead ership council.

On the day of the meeting, Queen Zawa's chief scientist, Karak, stood be fore Zawa and the council. "Queen Zawa, ladies and gentlemen of the council, I have important information that could affect the entire Kingdom of Athemba. My team of scientists has been monitoring the water level of the Mighty River. Our findings indicate that it is dropping quickly. The decline was slow at first, so slow that we would not have noticed without our monitoring equipment, but now it is growing more noticeable. We have evidence to suggest that this trend will not reverse itself. It will only become worse. Expansion in the kingdom has put great demands on the Mighty River."

With some concern, Queen Zawa asked, "So, how concerned should we be? What should we do?" Trying not to upset her too much, Karak told the Queen that more water must be directed into the Mighty River at its head, where it be gins. "But won't the waters from other sources in the kingdom dilute the magical qualities of the Mighty River?" the Queen asked.

As a child, she had been told many stories warning about the dangers of in troducing "different" water sources into the Mighty River. With a smile on his face Karak responded, "We thought so at first, so we conducted some tests. Our tests show there's something about the area where the Mighty River begins. Any water put in at that point also obtains magical qualities as it flows down the river." Karak continued with confidence, "So we must develop a system to direct other sources of water to the head of the Mighty River." The council members looked at each other with concern. Like everyone else in the kingdom, they grew up with the same stories the Queen heard.

"Are you positively sure this will not compromise the Mighty River?" asked Queen Zawa.

With even more confidence, Karak answered, "Yes, very sure! Our research is sound."

"This sounds like a big initiative, do we have the resources to do this?"

Karak paused to figure out how he would respond, "Well yes, but we will have to stop or cut back many of our current projects. We will need some of those resources to build an effective water diversion system." At this, many of the council members grumbled. They did not want to give up the projects cur rently underway, projects that made their life comfortable. "The system will take many years to build, so we must begin now," Karak warned. "If we do not start quickly, the entire kingdom will suffer irreversible consequences."

After hearing from Karak, the Queen gathered privately with her leadership council. "You've heard what Karak and the other scientists have said. You've seen their research. What do you think we should do?" One by one the council members gave their opinions. There was much debate.

Finally, the last council member took the floor. It was Mawni, Keeper of the Resources, and a trusted advisor to Zawa. "What Karak and his scientists have told us concerns me. It will be difficult, but we must be willing to give up some of the notions of our youth and accept the evidence before us." Referring to some notes he had written, Mawni continued, "But let's not panic. I propose we start developing some water conservation programs. This will give us time to plan and save resources for the water diversion system. For now, conserving water should become our main focus, our top priority."

After Mawni gave his opinion, Queen Zawa left the room to think. In private chambers next door, her majesty sat down to contemplate all the information she had just received. Never before had she faced such a severe challenge. In her gut, she did not want to believe all the things Karak said, though she knew he was right. After all, he is the Chief Scientist for a reason. Queen Zawa did not want to act too hastily and alarm her people. But her instincts told her that she needed to act soon.

Mawni's idea for water conservation programs was a good one. Growth in the kingdom was affecting the Mighty River, and if intentional efforts were not taken to address those changes, everyone would suffer. Her role as leader was to make tough decisions, to lead and inspire. She rejoined her leadership council and revealed what she had decided.

"We must communicate to our people that the problem we face with the Mighty River is serious. As Mawni has stated, it must become part of our main focus as a kingdom. If we do this right, the entire kingdom of Athemba will benefit for generations to come. If we fail, everyone will feel the harsh conse quences. We will send a notice to all the people of Athemba informing them of the situation. We will ask them to begin monitoring their water use, to find ways to conserve. And I will create a new office, the Office of Water, to monitor the situation, to oversee conservation programs and develop a plan for getting more water to the Mighty River." Zawa paused, holding up a cup of water before her, "We must take this situation seriously, but not let it deter us from the programs and activities that have made Athemba the most admired kingdom in the world." The council members clapped in agreement.

In the following months, the Office of Water sent notices to provincial leaders throughout the land. The leaders were asked to advise everyone in their jurisdic tion to find ways of using water more efficiently. They were told that informa tional sessions and workshops were being developed to teach water conservation methods. Finally, they were informed of a system being developed to ensure that the Mighty River would get all the water it needed. This last part shocked many of the leaders, who still believed the tales of what would happen if "different" waters were introduced into the Mighty River.

After nine months, Queen Zawa and the leadership council received a report from the Office of Water. The news was not good. Many people still believed that introducing "other" waters would weaken the Mighty River's magic. Few people attended the voluntary water conservation workshops. Hardly anyone conserved water. The report greatly dismayed Queen Zawa, so she brought her leadership council together and asked why the people of Athemba were not taking the situation more seriously. "We have made this a top priority in the kingdom, yet it has not become a top priority for our citizens. This is not like our people. Council members, where have we failed?"

Her request for input was greeted with a loud silence. "What's the problem?" she asked. Council members remained hesitant. As the silence continued, Queen Zawa's dismay grew into anger. Finally, a voice rang out from the back of the room. It was Zonka, a council member from an outer province. Ever since the water level from the Mighty River began to drop, his province had found it increasingly difficult to get water from the river.

"We in the outer provinces already are suffering from this crisis. We are greatly disappointed by the lack of leadership involved in the water conservation workshops. I have attended many workshops, but have seen few of my colleagues. Our lack of involvement is sending a message to our people. Why should they consider the matter of the Mighty River important when our actions tell them that we don't think it's important?" Zonka also told the Queen that the people of her province were losing respect for her.

"Why is this?" Zawa queried with great disappointment in her heart.

With some hesitancy Zonka responded, "They do not see you or your province doing anything to conserve water. And they have not heard of any progress on the plan to divert water to the Mighty River." This information both angered and embarrassed the Queen. She dismissed the council and told them to come back the next day. All that evening she wrestled with what had been said.

At the council meeting the next day, Queen Zawa asked the Director of the Office of Water about the progress being made with the long-range strategy. "We have made little progress Queen Zawa. Very few council members and provincial leaders have attended the strategic planning meetings. In addition, those in attendance have expressed a reluctance to provide resources for the water diversion system."

Queen Zawa gave piercing stares to each one of her council members, then asked the Director, "So why do you think this is happening?" The Director paused, unsure if she should speak her mind. "It's okay," Queen Zawa told the Director. "Please speak candidly."

With caution the Director began, "I can't be completely sure, but my guess is they, the council members and provincial leaders, do not truly believe in the system to divert water to the Mighty River. They have not taken the time to educate themselves on Dr. Karak's research, and thus they still hold onto the irrational tales they grew up with as children." The Director continued, then bit her tongue, feeling she had said enough.

"Is there more?" asked the angry Queen.

"And they don't want to take resources away from projects within their own provinces," the Director blurted out. "I told them that resources would not be taken away from the important projects, only from ones that seemed like luxu ries. They still were reluctant and…"

The Queen finished the Director's statement, "…and so people throughout Athemba observe their leaders' lack of action and involvement and deem the matter of the Mighty River unimportant."

"Yes, Queen Zawa, exactly."

Next, Queen Zawa called the leader of her province before the council. "Why are we not doing anything to use water more efficiently in our province? Weren't you and the other provincial leaders directed to do so?"

The provincial leader reacted with surprise. "I didn't put much stock in the notice sent out because nothing in it seemed to say action was urgent. Nothing was required. Everything was voluntary. And, I only received one notice. I know something is important when I get many notices from you." Trying to ease the discomfort in the air, he said with a hint of laughter, "There's no mistaking when something is important to the Queen and the leadership council. That's when the kingdom sees all of you involved and talking about the issue. And when something's really important, you require us to act. That's when I know I have to put the issue at the top of my agenda."

Seeing that the Queen was getting impatient, the provincial leader spoke more quickly, "And in the past, when something was very important, you called all the provincial leaders to the palace to discuss the issue and develop an integrated plan of attack, a strategy. Nothing like that happened this time. Yes, we were invited to meetings by the Office of Water, but…" he paused to glance at the Director, "…provincial leaders don't take invitations from low-level offices seri ously.

"Finally, when things are really important, you always placed the issue very high on the agenda in our provincial leader meetings. At our last meeting, the matter of the Mighty River was next to last order of business. We sat and listened to new techniques that were being developed to build homes faster. We listened as Chief Scientist Karak introduced his plan for saving some of the animals that had been leaving the province. One agenda item after another, we listened. Many provincial leaders could not help but think that the water problem was not a sub stantive issue."

Queen Zawa had heard enough. She understood what was happening. She and her leadership council had said that saving the Mighty River was an important issue, but did little to communicate that importance. They did not model the be havior they expected of others. Queen Zawa was greatly disappointed in herself. She always had made it a point to align her actions with her words. It was a mat ter of integrity and credibility for her.

She thought back to what she had done to communicate the gravity of the matter, and recalled attending only one water conservation workshop…to kick it off. She didn't even stay for the entire workshop. "What must I have commu nicated to those at the workshop," she said to herself. "I haven't even attended a strategic planning session to develop an integrated plan to save the river." She tried to excuse herself with the thought that she'd been busy with other projects and activities, but she couldn't. She had made it known that the Mighty River was an important issue. "If the Mighty River is not even on my agenda, I can't expect it to be on others' agendas." She knew what she had to do.

Queen Zawa called a gathering of the entire kingdom. On the day of the assembly, she stood before the citizens of Athemba, "People of Athemba, I have called us together today because we have an opportunity to do something that will benefit our entire kingdom for generations to come. What we do now will call for changes that many of us will find uncomfortable, but these changes will ensure that the Mighty River will thrive long into the future. And when the Mighty River thrives, we also thrive as a people. I am asking everyone to take part in the initiatives that will be developed, and to be accountable to one another for the success of these initiatives."

A voice rang out from the crowd, "Does this mean you and the leadership council will be accountable, too?" There was a deafening silence as everyone looked to see how Queen Zawa would react. Some people began to move toward the man who called out the question.

"Leave this man alone," the Queen commanded. "His question is a good one in light of our recent actions as your leaders. Or should I say, lack of actions. Yes, we have failed you and we apologize. You have told me that you respect me in large part because I am a leader with integrity. I always have led by example. But this time my example has been poor. I could try to make excuses by saying that I am busy with kingdom issues, but that only would say to you that the Mighty River is not a kingdom issue."

Looking toward the leadership council the Queen continued, "The council and I now are restating to all of you that the Mighty River is a kingdom issue. You can expect all of us to act accordingly. When we do not, we expect you to tell us. From our actions you should be able to see that we believe the Mighty River is a top priority. We no longer can use mere effort as a measure of our success. We cannot stop at good intentions. Success must be our measure of success. Accepting mediocrity on this issue says the issue is unimportant. And anything less than success will hurt all of us, not just some of us." Many citizens in the crowd began to cheer their approval.

"So I ask you once again to do your part in future efforts. The journey will be a long one and there will be failures along the way. Errors will be made, as you already have seen. But our efforts should be seen as a journey of error correction. Are we together on this?" Now, more in the crowd voiced their support.

A lone voice pierced the excitement, "But what are we going to do?" The deafening silence returned.

"That is yet to be seen. But if we move forward together with a sense of unified purpose, with clarity about what is truly important and with the under standing that all of Athemba will prosper if we are successful, then I know that whatever we do will be the right thing to do." Again, the people cheered.

"And in difficult times, in times when we experience failure, in times when we are disappointed with the actions of our fellow brothers and sisters, it is in those times that we should recall what my good friend once told me." The Queen paused, the crowd eagerly awaiting her next words. "When I first became your Queen, my friend, Thaccis, told me, 'Go out and communicate your message to the people of Athemba...and if all else fails, use words. It's your actions and not your words that your people will most believe."

At this all the citizens of Athemba erupted with thunderous clapping and cheering. The people left the gathering with great momentum and a sense of renewed hope   hope in their Queen, in their leadership and in themselves.

Progress always involves risk; you can't steal second base and keep your foot on first.
~ Frederick Wilcox ~

22
Swimming's Great, Just Don't Get Me Wet

THERE I was being a dutiful dad watching my son learn how to swim. Zachary has been taking swim lessons on and off for the past year. Now, as a 4 year old (oops, 4 and a half year old…he reminds me often of this important distinction) he is starting to prove that little people do not necessarily sink in a watery environment. Don't get me wrong, no one observing him would compare him to an Olympic swimmer, but the signs are there.

But this story is not about Zachary. It's about the swim teacher that was running a class at the other end of the pool. She stood at the edge with a towel wrapped around her waist and took attendance. Her class was filled with kids that looked a little older than Zachary, probably 5 or 6 years old. It was obvious that they too had not mastered the art of swimming yet, but they were a little further on their journey than my son.

As I watched Zachary in his lesson, I glanced over at this other class to see if it would be appropriate for my son's next stage of training. What surprised me as I watched wasn't that the kids flailed in the water like hooked fish, but that the swim teacher had not joined them in the pool. She continued to stand on the side, barking out instructions, "Long arms, reach and pull…1, 2, 3, 4, breath, reach and pull." The instruction sounded good, like she knew what she was talking about. Surely, she soon would jump into the pool to offer more detailed instruc tion and to model the right techniques.

As I continued to watch, part of me wanted to go over and push the teacher in. Fifteen minutes into the lesson, she remained dry. Now, instead of being perplexed, I was getting impressed by this new method. "What a novel idea," I thought, teaching swimming from afar without getting wet. When one of her students needed some assistance, she walked over, knelt down and made some motions showing what she wanted the student to do. That towel remained around her waist; she was still dry. Clearly, the teacher had no intention of entering the pool on this particular day, and I began to wonder: "Was there something wrong with her today? Did her doctor tell her not to get wet? Does she know how to swim?"

I suppose swimming can be taught without getting wet, but I never saw that method when I learned how to swim, nor did those teaching my son take that approach. I couldn't make sense of it. It might make a little sense if the students were more accomplished swimmers that did not require as much instruction, but this definitely was not the case.

Teaching swimming to beginners without getting in the water, without getting in the environment, seems counterintuitive to me. While it may work to some degree, it does not seem like the most effective method of instruction. It does not seem like it would produce the best outcome.

With this swim teacher in mind, I pose these questions to all of us responsible for diversity initiatives in our organizations: Is this how some key people in your organization, especially leaders, approach diversity? Can you see signs that your organization wants to "swim," but doesn't want to dive in?

Often, when the "swim, but don't get wet" approach is taken, diversity and inclusion initiatives are seen as "extracurricular" rather than integral to the daily operations and growth of a company. It produces a "to do list" mentality, where actions tend to be seen as separate, unconnected events...definitely not strategic. Moreover, when times get tough economically, diversity initiatives are among the first in line at the chopping block. So take a critical look at your diversity initiatives to see if they might need a push into the pool. A "let's get wet" com mitment is crucial to the success of any diversity initiative. And when I say wet, I mean fully immersed, not just "feet in the water" wet. Anything less allows us to feel good and to stay comfortable, but does little to produce desired outcomes.

Ready to jump in? The initial entry may not feel that great. But stay a while and you'll likely find the waters of diversity to be quite refreshing.

When every physical and mental resource is focused, one's power to solve a problem multiplies tremendously.
~ Norman Vincent Peale ~

23
The Power of Magnification

WHEN I was a youngster growing up in California, I spent much of my summer vacation playing outside. For some reason, I had a lot of interest in nature and science, so I caught a lot of bugs and insects that found themselves in my path. Up until my seventh birthday I was relatively nice to the bugs that I captured. Yes, occasionally I would "mishandle" a bug to the point that it would die, or I would turn an eight legged creature into a six legged one. But heck, why be a little kid if you can't experiment with bugs? Though I held a number of funerals for the little creatures that didn't survive my operating table, for the most part I took the Hippocratic oath of "do no harm" rather seriously. That is, until I turned seven.

On my seventh birthday I received something I vaguely recall as a "science kit." This thing was cool to a 7-year old. Heck, it would be cool to a 37-year-old. It had a microscope, tweezers, plastic test tubes and a bunch of other things. But what I really liked was the magnifying glass. I remember thinking whoever invented this thing must have been a genius. With a magnifying glass I could make a little Oreo cookie look huge. The cookie didn't fill up my tummy any better, but it looked like it would. I could see the tiniest details on my dog's face. Hair follicles sure look funny up close. But the best thing was examining the bugs that I caught. If you've ever seen a grasshopper's head up close you can understand the pure joy such a sight can give a 7 year old.

My wrong turn down the road of bug cruelty began several days after my birthday. It was, like usual, a hot and sunny day in Southern California. I thought, "what a great day to go outside with my new magnifying glass to look for bugs." Little did I know my fall from bug grace was close at hand. Unfortunately for the potato bugs that lived under a board at the side of our apartment, I began with them. All I wanted to do was look at the bugs up close. If you think potato bugs are ugly to the naked eye, wait 'til you get them under a magnifying glass. It's a good ugly though.

A curious thing happened as I examined the potato bugs. With one big one under scrutiny, I pulled my head away to peer at another creature and, in doing so, let the sun shine into the magnifying glass. It put a nice little spotlight on the bug, and, as I tried to focus once again on the bug, I saw that the spotlight got bigger or smaller depending on the distance between the magnifying glass and the bug. I also noticed that as the spotlight got smaller, there was much more movement by the bug. I pursued this newfound correlation with great interest.

Eventually, after a series of adjustments, I had a highly concentrated, bright dot on the bug. Soon after, smoke began rising from the creature, accompanied by a slight sizzling sound. The bug's hurried movements to get away told me that this was not an enjoyable experience, but I followed with my magnifying glass anyway, and it did not take long for the bug to stop moving. With the light still concentrated on the back of the bug, it caught fire. "Way cool!" I looked around to make sure my mother was not seeing her son's metamorphosis into Mr. Hyde.

I spent what seemed like hours finding and roasting bugs...then my mom found me. Suffice it to say, that was the end of my bug burning days. How can life be fair when 7 year olds can't enjoy a day in the sun with bugs and a magni fying glass? Melting plastic Army men would have to do.

The lesson here comes from the power of a magnifying glass focusing light onto an object. The magnifying glass takes incoherent or "unorganized" light particles and directs them in such a way that a very tight, concentrated and pow erful beam is produced. What results is a laser of light that can produce a lot of damage. Without a magnifying glass or other similar tool, light particles remain unorganized, diffused and weak.

Do the last three adjectives more or less describe your organization's diver sity initiatives? I often have observed that when organizations try to address every possible dimension of diversity (because they don't want to "leave anyone out"), they dilute the entire process and rarely get anything done. In fact, what sometimes happens is that they do so much that they become satisfied in the "doing" and put little emphasis on the "outcome." Or what else can happen is that employees latch onto a particular dimension of diversity with which they are most comfortable and use it as a proxy for being comfortable with all dimen sions. For example, someone who fully embraces gender diversity might think - falsely - that they are "okay" with all dimensions of diversity, when in fact they have not come to grips with race diversity, sexual orientation or religion. If they think this way, they rarely see the value of committing themselves to an organization's diversity efforts.

By emphasizing one or two dimensions of diversity, an organization can "fo cus" its resources and do much more "damage" than with a diffused approach. Does this mean that an organization forgets about other dimensions of diversity? Absolutely not! It means that the organization has a primary focus on one or two dimensions that it has deemed vitally important, while still addressing other inclusion issues.

Different organizations may have different areas of focus. Some, based on research and changing demographics, might say that gender diversity will be most important. Others, based on their location, might choose racial/ethnic di versity. Still more may choose generational diversity because of the make up of their workforce. Great care must be taken to communicate the rationale behind emphasizing certain dimensions of diversity, the same way an organization com municates that it will focus on a particular aspect of its business…like customer service over marketing. This does not mean marketing will be completely for gotten. Rather, it says that at this particular time the data suggest that customer satisfaction needs greater attention if the entire organization expects to be suc cessful in the future.

If your organization is committed to diversity and inclusion, it may help to think of exclusion and discrimination as big, ugly bugs. In doing so, you can think of your strategic diversity plan as a big magnifying glass that either can put a diffused spotlight on the ugliness of all the bugs (and nothing else), or can focus resources to obliterate the bugs one by one. Why have a weak and diffused approach to diversity and inclusion when you can leverage the power of focus and magnification?

Most people never run far enough on their first wind, to find out if they've got a second. Give your dreams all you've got and you'll be amazed at the energy that comes out of you.

~ William James ~

24
Nubby Sandals

WE recently welcomed a newborn into our home. Natalie is our fourth child, and bringing her home brought back a lot of great memories. But in bringing her home, we also ushered out something we hold dearly...sleep! As newborn babies go, Natalie has been quite good. But she does have her moments (or hours) when she likes to punish mom and dad for nine months of cramped living space. One of those moments occurred last week.

Mom had just fed Natalie around 11:00 p.m. and it was bedtime. At least, it was our bedtime. Natalie had other plans. Because she cannot verbalize her thoughts, Natalie summons mom and dad in other ways, a method we refer to in English as "crying." Being the thoughtful dad and husband that I am, I took my turn with Natalie.

When our previous kids cried as newborns, I took them for a nice car ride or a walk. This time I thought I'd combine the two and take a trip to the local grocery store that is open all night. As I headed out the door, I was unable to find my sandals so I squeezed into my wife's. They looked like ordinary sandals, but they felt uniquely good. These particular sandals had a bunch of little nubs in the sole that are designed to stimulate the bottom of your foot. And they did a good job of it. So, with a couple of stimulated feet I went off with Natalie to take our midnight ride and walk.

As I pushed Natalie around the store I thought about how nice my feet felt wearing my wife's sandals. Whoever thought of placing those tiny little nubs in the soles was a genius. I even thought about sending a letter to the manufacturer to tell them how good it feels. But that was a fleeting thought.

Ten minutes in the store turned into 20 minutes. At about this time, I began noticing the sandals again. Those little nubs started to hurt a little. The more I walked, the more they hurt. And after more than 50 minutes of walking around the store, my feet were killing me...all because of those nubs. Fortunately, by this time Natalie had fallen asleep so I could go home and take those nubby sandals off.

The next day, I told my wife about my midnight trip to the store with Natalie, and asked her how she could walk in those things for so long. "They hurt me at first, too," she replied matter-of-factly, "but I kept wearing them and pretty soon not only didn't they hurt, they actually felt good." I told her I'd stick with my nub less sandals.

After thinking about this experience a little, I realized that this is how many people initially experience "diversity." Many well-meaning people get passion ate about diversity and want to do something right away. They participate in a workshop or go to an inspiring conference. They feel good about what they are doing, as they should. But then the honeymoon feeling wears off, the new toy luster fades and the work really begins.

Being intentional about experiencing and understanding different people and cultures is difficult. For example, making a point of using diverse suppliers is not easy. Saying something when a co worker makes an "I didn't mean anything by it" racial joke is tough. These actions are like those nubby sandals - they hurt. Are you and your organization willing to proceed through the pain? Are you prepared to be diligent after the "easy stuff" passes? Are you willing to walk not just one mile, but hundreds of miles in another's shoes? Sometimes the first mile is the easy one. It's what follows that too many people and organizations are unwilling to journey upon. But if you are committed, the rewards can be many.

So take a walk in those nub-filled diversity sandals. But before you set off on the journey, know that there will be pain involved. Also know that those who stick it out will reap the rewards that diversity offers.

Human progress is furthered, not by conformity, but by aberration.
~ H.L. Mencken ~

25
Two Pairs Better Than One?

IF you were to open my sock drawer you might think I actually have four feet instead of the standard allotment of two. My socks easily fill up a whole drawer. Okay, two drawers. I have tube socks, ankle socks, Argyle print socks, hiking socks that wick moisture, extra length dress socks, 100% cotton socks, cotton/poly blend socks, blue ones, black ones...you get the picture, I have lots of socks. No, I don't have a sock fetish. Nor do I collect socks. I don't even believe there will be a sock shortage in the future. (Although I'd be prepared if one ever oc curred.) Our current dryer, unlike our previous one, doesn't seem to have a Black Hole that arbitrarily sucks away one sock from every matching pair.

I have a very good reason for owning an unusually large collection of socks. And it all has to do with comfort. I have narrow, bony feet that require extra padding so they fit snugly in the "average" men's D-width shoe. It all started when I first began wearing adult-size shoes. I knew something wasn't right the first time I put on a pair. The length of the shoe was correct, but my feet were, as the sales person said, "swimming" in the toe area. She suggested I pull the laces tight, bringing the sides together to reduce the effective width of the shoe. I did. It didn't help. I still was swimming even though the sides were as close as they were going to get.

Despite the not so perfect fit, I begged my mom to get me the shoes. They were, after all, what all the cool guys at school were wearing. I didn't want to be left behind when the cool train left the station. But my mom wasn't so sure about purchasing shoes that didn't fit. She warned me that they could give me blisters because they were so wide. I didn't listen, and after making my case for the absolute necessity of these shoes, my mother caved. The shoes were mine.

Several weeks and one painful blister later, I began to buy into the saying, "Mothers know best." Not once, though, did my mom say, "I told you so." That was not her way. She analyzed my predicament objectively and quickly came up with a solution. She suggested I wear an extra pair of socks to fill in the extra space in the shoes. I resisted, telling her no other kids I knew wore two pairs of socks. She told me I had two options: I could wear two pairs of socks, or she would buy me women's shoes that are narrower. I started wearing two pairs of socks.

It felt funny, almost unnatural the first time I put on two pairs of socks. But as soon as I placed my feet into my once too wide and painful shoes, I couldn't fathom why anyone would want to wear just one pair. I knew I would never go back. The extra cushioning and better fit put me in a state of sock Nirvana. Questions filled my head: "Why hadn't I done this before? How'd my mom get so smart? Why do people pierce their belly buttons?" Questions unanswerable, but worthy of examination.

At first I tried to hide my two-pair addiction from others, but my fellow basketball team members found me out. I became the target of locker room jokes, but I didn't care. The comfort of my feet was more important than conforming to one pair culture. I wore two pairs of socks all the time, even in the triple digit heat of summer. To this day I continue to wear two pairs of socks. And yes, I still get questions and ribbing from my friends, especially when they see my white tube socks peaking out from under dark dress socks. I, as a "multi-pair" person, am concerned more with the health of my feet than the perceptions of others.

Does your organization have a "one-pair" culture that "two-pair" people find uncomfortable, or do not "fit" into well? While the mainstream norm of "one pair" has worked relatively well for years, more "two-pair" and "multi-pair" people are on the not so distant horizon. Organizations that do not recognize the coming wave of "two-pairers" will be unable to compete with those that are creating a culture that embraces one pairers, two pairers and even three pairers.

Multi pair society is where we are headed. Is your organization ready to go there, too? Or will your organization remain stuck in the old "one pair-adigm." If it's the latter, all the data and evidence suggest you better get "unstuck." Two-pairs, three pairs and other multi pairs are not necessarily better than one, but they will be part of the mix. Make sure your "organizational sock drawer" embraces all kinds. It will be more comfortable for everyone in the long run.

We can't make people better by trying to eliminate their weaknesses, but we can help then perform better by building on their strengths.
~ Peter Drucker ~

26
Cool Features

THOSE who've been around me long enough know that I'm somewhat of a "tech hound." I regularly sniff out new electronic gadgets, always wanting to own the latest and greatest. A little while ago I bought a new Compaq IPAQ PDA. For those who are technology laggards, PDA stands for "personal digital assistant." At the time of purchase, it was the sleekest, fastest, most powerful PDA around. I am a technology "early adopter," which means I'm not smart enough to wait several months for prices to go down and bugs to be fixed.

My IPAQ has a 206Mhz Intel StrongARM RISC processor, 64 MB RAM, 32MB ROM, a color-reflective TFT LCD with 65,000 colors, a Secure Digital Card expansion slot (as opposed to the non secure ones you can get), Integrated Bluetooth Technology and a bunch of other features that are too numerous to mention. I could tell you what all this means, but then I'd have to kill you. Trust me, this thing is cool. Besides holding my planner and calendar, it also stores names, addresses and telephone numbers. They tell me I can connect to the Web with my IPAQ PDA. I also can use it as a GPS unit (I could tell ya, but I'd have to...) and alarm clock. I can run slideshows, store and listen to MP3's and beam data to a printer. I believe it also serves as a kitchen sink, though I have yet to find the button for that particular transformation. Did I mention this thing is cool?

The first time I pulled my IPAQ out at a meeting, the people around me drooled in envy. I often strive for humility, but this was too much. Yes, bow to me you late adopters. Just to rub it in, I reached in my bag and pulled out a rather small, black, shiny box. I pressed a couple of buttons and began to open the rectangular gadget. Before their very eyes opened a miniature, James Bondish keyboard for my IPAQ. Feeling like the only kid on the block with a brand spankin' new bike, I connected my IPAQ to the keyboard and began typing. Nothing important, but that's not the point. I was typing!

Since that heavenly day I have not used that keyboard again, just like the vast majority of features Compaq designers so brilliantly included in my PDA. I don't connect to the Web with it. I don't use its GPS features to find my way. I don't even illegally download music off the 'Net. I could, but I don't, and not because it's against the law. About 99.99 percent of the time I use my IPAQ to remind me of things I should be doing, and to get the phone numbers for people who can help me with the things I should be doing. That's right. I use a $600 gadget for something a $10 paper based planner can do. Okay, I do use its alarm clock feature, something my previous Franklin planner didn't have. So I really do feel better about spending all that money.

Could I be more efficient if I took advantage of all the IPAQ's diverse fea tures? Yes. Do I want to take the time and go through the "hassle" of learning about all those features? No. I think all those gadgets are cool and I know many are of great use, but I just don't seem to find the time to travel up the steep learn ing curve. I brag about having all those features, but I have yet to put the majority to use - to help me get more work done, to be more efficient…to be better. Nope, I just use my IPAQ to remind me of meetings and phone numbers.

As I think about how I underutilize the diverse features of my PDA, it makes me think about the many organizations that underutilize the talent and skills within their own walls because they've "branded" people by race, gender, age, etc. For example, a company might hire a very talented marketer, who happens to be Asian, and then expect that person to develop marketing plans only targeted at Asian groups. While that person may or may not be skilled at marketing to Asian groups, limiting the job to "Asian" products neglects ideas and solutions that might apply to marketing efforts in many areas. Also, there are many organiza tions that place great value on what some call "male attributes" (aggressiveness, competitiveness, individuality) and thus punish (intentionally and unintention ally) those who might show "female attributes" (cooperation, group-orientation, nurturing) because they are seen as weaknesses. An organization's inability to embrace the strengths found in all of its people will prevent it from taking advan tage of opportunities that require different ways of viewing the world.

Taking steps to create a diverse workforce is one thing. Doing away with old structures and traditional methods so a diverse workforce can excel is quite another. It takes time, some "hassle" and patience to transform traditional struc tures into cultures that can take advantage of existing and potential diversity.

Organizations that work through the pain of transformation will leverage the strength of diversity to its fullest.

I will be taking my own advice and learning more about how to use the many features of my IPAQ. It will take some time, but I am making a conscious effort to do so.

And did I mention I just got the newest Motorola cell phone? It's got a lot of cool features.

Until lions get their own historians, tales of the hunt will always
glorify the hunter.
~ African Proverb ~

27
Recording Errors

IF you own a relatively new computer, the system you have probably allows you to write data onto a compact disc or DVD. Heck, even the computer I pur chased several years ago has a nifty CD writer that lets me digitally record my favorite songs onto disc. Though I thought this was pretty cool technology when I bought my computer, I hadn't put it to use until recently.

It was a wonderfully calm Saturday afternoon at our house. I remember the calmness well because with four children (all under eight years old) this rare phenomenon occurs at Haley's Comet intervals. And it only happened this time because somehow the stars and moon aligned and all the kids were napping. I remember asking my wife to bottle whatever she did to get them all simultane ously into a nearly comatose state. "Already did it," she joked, pointing to a newly purchased bottle of cough medicine on the counter. No, we don't dope our kids...though sometimes, er, often times I've wanted to. But back to the calm afternoon.

I wanted to do something special with the few blessed hours of peace and quiet. So I proceeded to do what I had been wanting to do for years...make a CD of songs that would transport me romantically back to my younger days. Ahh, the thought of having some of my favorite 80's hits all on one CD gave me goose bumps, though I couldn't rule out the possibility that our cold basement was the source of those bumps.

I went to my music collection and starting pulling out the CD's that I would use. Little River Band, Boston, Hall and Oates, Bruce Hornsby and the Range, Billy Joel, Culture Club (yes, I have a Culture Club CD), Starship, REO Speed wagon, Ambrosia, The Village People (everybody has this disc for one song, right?), Luther Vandross...even the Bee Gees! I was in music heaven. After mak ing a list of my favorite songs, I began recording. The CD writer seemed to work well, and it was rather easy. I quickly got the system down and really didn't have to think about the process. All the songs were recording nicely.

Several hours later I finished my "Younger Days Compilation." Amazingly, my kids were still asleep. I wondered if my wife wasn't joking about the cough medicine. Didn't matter to me as I eagerly took my newly completed CD master piece and put it into my stereo system. Sitting back, I listened with utter delight. As the songs played, I asked if there could be anything musically better than "hits from the 80's." I told my wife I was in music Nirvana. She checked to make sure I hadn't overdosed on the cough medicine.

But I was rocked from my heavenly state in the middle of Toto's hit, "Rosan na," by the repeating "d-d-d-d-d" sound that CD's make when they're dirty or scratched. It lasted no more than a couple seconds and shouldn't have bothered me, but it did. A perfect "80's" CD ruined. I took the CD out of the player and checked for a scratch or dirt. I couldn't find any, but I cleaned the CD just in case and put it back into the player. Listening to "Rosanna" again, I hoped for the best. But there it was again, "d-d-d-d-d," in the same exact spot. I cleaned the CD again, this time with the special stuff you can get to clean CD's. Hoping against hope that the CD was just dirty, I played "Rosanna" again. The haunting "d-d-d-d-d" was still there. Now I was sure that the CD wasn't dirty. Something must have happened during the recording process that I did not notice. It was a faulty recording. The CD was only playing what was burned into it. It could do nothing else.

In some wacky ways our brains are like CD's. Over the course of our lives the things we see, hear and smell are "burned" into our brain. In fact, data are being written onto our brains on a continuous basis. Some of that information is being "burned in" with our complete awareness, other information is recorded without us really knowing. It doesn't matter how the data get there, and it doesn't even matter if the data are "good." Our brains use that information to develop the lenses through which we interpret the world around us, including the people in that world. What we have in our brains influences the way we see people, the way we interpret other incoming information, the manner in which we make decisions, etc. If we have "bad" data or incomplete information (as a result of a "skip" or "scratch" in the recording process) then our actions based on that data potentially are erroneous.

Here's where we have to be honest with ourselves in analyzing the informa tion we've received about people different from ourselves. Think about what you learned in your everyday world about women. How might that form your opin ions about what roles women should have? Critically analyze the media you ab sorb, whether it is television, magazines, billboards or newspapers. Ask yourself how people of color are depicted, for example. How might those thousands of images your brain has recorded affect the way you see, treat and react to people of color? If you go to church, mosque or synagogue, critically ask yourself how your place of worship thinks about and treats people with a different sexual orientation than the majority. How might that impact the way you think about and treat them? Think about how you grew up. Did you have a lot of diverse experiences that put you in contact with diverse peoples? Or did you have very few interactions with "different" people? If you did not have a lot of experiences that put you face to face with people diversity, assess how that might affect your current thinking about diversity issues.

Data from all these sources influence your thinking at some level, whether you want to admit it or not. Your diversity experiences, or lack thereof, burns information into your brain. Your reactions to others and their behaviors are a direct result of all that data you've picked up over the years. Like the CD that only can play what was written onto to it, whether good or bad, you only can act according to what's in your brain. You can't expect to be unbiased or non dis criminatory toward others if the information you have about them is biased and discriminatory. Makes sense, doesn't it?

I'm sure you have heard people say things like, "I don't have a biased bone in my body" or "I'm colorblind, I treat everyone the same." Maybe even you have uttered such things. Have you ever considered how accurate (or inaccurate) these statements are, in light of how human beings actually gather and utilize informa tion. If you can come to a better understanding of the information you have about others and the authenticity of that data, you will have taken many steps forward in living and excelling in an increasingly diverse world. Remember, much like a CD recording, you tend to only "play back" what you've been given.

And it's also important to understand that you'll never really be able to erase the "bad" information in your head. It's burned in there rather permanently, like a CD. But you can teach yourself to be more mindful of how that "bad" infor mation affects your daily actions, reactions and decision making. You can learn how to manage the "bad" information that exists in your head. You also can become more aware of your "gut reactions" to people different from yourself, and can question those reactions knowing that they likely are based on stereo types and biased images. Indeed, a major shift in diversity training focuses on helping people understand and manage their biases, because we know we can't completely get rid of our prejudices. They always will be there, and if we aren't aware of them they might rear their ugly heads at the worst times. It's not neces sarily about intentionality.

Back to my CD and that calm day. My wife suggested I re record the song. I reminded her that the system I have does not allow me to re write CD's, so she then suggested that I make a new disc. I could have done that, but I'm one of those people who likes to do it right the first time. And plus, it would be wasting 70 minutes of other great songs on the CD. Besides, the kids were awakening from their slumber, and my wife had taken the cough medicine. I would have to listen to the CD as is, to help remind me that "recording errors" are a fact of life, and life, as someone once told me, is a process of "error correction."

Courage is not the absence of fear, but rather the judgment that something else is more important than one's fear.
~ Ambrose Redmoon ~

28
A Bigger Pie

MY oldest son, Nicholas, loves Oreo cookies. Let me qualify that. Like many other Oreo lovers, he is most passionate not about the entire cookie, but the creamy middle. If there is an Oreo anywhere near, Nicholas no doubt will be among the first to make claim.   Such was the case during a recent family dinner.

Like many families concerned about the decline of the family, we make it a point to sit down together for dinner. It gives us time to talk about our day and build family unity without distractions. And fortunately for us, the cooking staff at the restaurant was a little slow giving us even more family time around the "dinner table."

Back to the Oreo. Nicholas had finished a very healthy dinner consisting of a hot dog and French fries when the dessert menu caught his eye. There, pictured before him was this 7 year old's Holy Grail, a vanilla sundae topped off with two Oreo cookies. No need to look at the rest of the menu, he knew what he wanted. The waitress seemed to know it, too. Obviously an Oreo lover herself, they shared an unspoken language, the act of ordering was accomplished without words.

His eyes lit up like fireflies on a warm summer night as the waitress brought out his sundae. He launched an all out assault on the cookies that lay helpless on top. But just as he reached for the first Oreo, a voice from across the table interrupted him. "Can I have an Oreo, Nicholas?" His younger brother had fired a verbal challenge to Nicholas' sense of brotherly love. Silence blanketed the table as Nicholas paused to measure his brother's request. I waited anxiously to see if my wife and I had raised a son who put others ahead of himself.

After what seemed like minutes, Nicholas negotiated creatively, "Jacob, how 'bout you have the outside after I eat the white stuff inside?" I'm sure his polite ness masked a wish that his parents had taken birth control more seriously fol lowing his own arrival into the world.

His brother would not settle for just part of an Oreo. In his mind, an Oreo does not have parts. It's just one whole cookie, and that's what he wanted. He restated his plea with a pathetic cry. Nicholas looked to me hoping I would intervene on his behalf. But as a Star Trek fan, I stayed true to the Prime Directive; I would not interfere in the lives of these lower life forms we call children. Besides, watching Nicholas struggle with an obvious moral dilemma was getting to be fun.

"But Jacob, if I give you the whole cookie, I'll only have one left," Nicholas tried to reason with his brother. He had not realized that younger brothers are not rational beings. Higher life forms actually might care about how another feels, but it was quite clear that this one had not yet evolved to that point. After minutes of pleading, the good in Nicholas broke through...kind of. "Okay, you can have the cookie. But I get one of yours next time." Nicholas handed an Oreo to his brother, and somberly began eating his remaining cookie.

As he finished his cookie, the waitress came by and asked Nicholas what was wrong. She had been watching from afar. Nicholas was in no mood to talk, but he responded anyway, "I only got one Oreo cookie." She got closer to Nicholas and told him she saw how nice he was to his brother. And as she commended him for sharing with a pat on the head, she pulled out two more Oreo cookies and put them on the table in front of him. The light returned to his eyes. He softly thanked his newfound Oreo angel and turned to me, "Look dad, she gave me two more Oreo's. I gave my brother a cookie and I got two back."

"That's cool!" I said, putting out my hand to receive a high-five.

Nicholas wound up and smacked my hand. "Yep, real cool," he replied. "You're right dad, sharing is a good thing."

Sharing is a good thing...what a wonderful lesson for a child to learn. It's also a great lesson for adults to learn and put into practice.

Often times, people view "diversity and inclusion" as a zero-sum endeavor. That is, there are finite "goodies" out there and giving up some of those "good ies" means that they'll have fewer "goodies" to enjoy. For some, sharing power and control and allowing others in on the decision making process only means, "I will have less." In other words, if I give up 10 percent of the "pie," that means I have less "pie." What these same people don't see or understand is that giving up 10 percent of the pie might help the pie grow. The resulting pie is now big ger. And though one might own a smaller percentage of a larger pie, it might be greater in size than a larger percentage of a smaller pie.

Allowing more, diverse people to be utilized where they previously were not included will bring advantages to organizations in an increasingly diverse future. Organizations that handle diversity strategically (read: share the pie for all to benefit) will have a great advantage over those that do not. Likely, they will grow while others will stagnate.

Too much energy put into preserving one's own power often has the ironic effect of endangering the enterprise that provides the power in the first place. Put that enterprise in enough danger because the leadership is not willing to share and include, and it ultimately will decline, if not disintegrate. I would argue that sharing control of a healthy, dynamic ship is much better than having total control of a sickly, sinking one. As my son would attest, 75 percent of four Oreo cookies is "real cool" compared to 100 percent of two Oreo cookies. Truly, sharing is a good thing.

When the system is broken, and all our efforts are directed at fixing individuals and not the system, we guarantee ourselves that we will always have individuals to fix.

~ Steve L. Robbins ~

29
It's the System Stupid

"DAD, there's bees in the house!" my son shouted from downstairs. I leisurely made my way down to our family room, not at all expecting to see any yellow- and black-striped insects buzzing around. I figured my 2-year-old son was referring to the Pooh video he was watching. When I got there, I noticed that my son was not watching the video. Instead, he was intently fixed on our ceiling lights.

"Whatcha looking at Jacob?" I asked.

"The bees. There's bees up there."   I looked up but didn't see anything. Being a good father and wanting to do what all those "be a good father" books tell me to do, I played along to encourage my child's imagination.

"Wow, Jacob, there are bees, lots of them." He looked at me quizzically.

"Not lots dad, just two. See," he said, pointing to a specific light in our ceiling. "Just two."

Again, I looked up but didn't see anything. I continued to play along, "Yep, just two." I walked over to my son to give him a hug. Good fathers do that, you know.   As I reached down to hug him, I heard a faint buzzing noise from above.

"Must be God telling me I was being a good father," I thought. Then, the buzzing got louder. I looked up to see what appeared to be a bee flying around our family room. My son saw it too, and barked out orders, "Get the kill bugger! Get the kill bugger!"

I jumped to my feet. "What's a kill bugger?"

"You know, a kill bugger," he replied. "Mommy uses it to dead the bees."

Thoughts raced through my head, "Kill bugger, mommy, bees, golf season's almost over." Then, it magically clicked. I made a major code break. "Yes, I'll go get the fly swatter," I exclaimed.

I rushed upstairs to get the "kill bugger," and a long-sleeved shirt and a pair of gloves. I wanted to protect myself from a bee that's one one thousandth of my size. It never dawned on me that I had left my son downstairs nearly naked, wearing only a pair of shorts. That's me being a good father again.

With full armor and the "kill bugger" in my hand, I ran downstairs to find the bee. Within minutes, I located my prey, which had brought friends. With two quick, surgical swats (okay, maybe five or six) I showed those bees why humans are atop the food chain. As a rite of passage, I handed my son the "kill bugger" and let him take a couple swats at the bees that lay motionless on our carpet. With the hunt over, my son helped me dispose of the unfortunate creatures.

I walked upstairs to put away the "kill bugger" and wondered how the bees had entered our house. "Maybe they just flew in when a door was kept opened," I thought. But my son mentioned that "mommy" had "dead" other bees.

I asked my wife if she had killed other bees, and she told me she had done so on several occasions in the past week. She figured they were coming through some vent in the basement, but hadn't had time to check her theory.

Believing my wife would take care of the "bee situation," I didn't give it another thought. At least, not until the next day when I had to pull out the "kill bugger" for another assignment. And again the next day, and the day after that, and the day after that. It was kind of fun at first, but after the fifth day I was get ting perturbed. That's how good fathers get when things don't go our way. We don't get angry or mad, just perturbed.

This went on for several weeks. The bees kept coming in, one by one, and every day I carved a few more notches onto the "kill bugger." It definitely no longer was fun now, especially since my 7 year old gave me a lecture about how bees are harmless and necessary. There goes the Father of the Year award.

I pictured my kids going into a post office to see their dad's unshaven face on the wall with a caption exclaiming, "Wanted, Bee Killer!" I decided to look for that vent to spare myself and the bees future grief.

After several hours of searching I found what I believed to be the breach in se curity. It had to be the radon gas tube that runs from our basement to the outside. I covered the tube, which allows potentially deadly radon gas to escape, with a mesh screen. Since that time we've not had to go on any more bee hunts.

Reflecting on this ordeal, I realized that the bees were just doing what bees do, flying around looking for food and plants to pollinate. The problem was the tube that allowed the bees to enter our house. Unfortunately, about 20 bees became innocent victims before I figured out the "issue" was not with the bees, but with the way our house was built, its structure.

Similarly, organizations sometimes mistakenly rush to conclude that perfor mance problems are the fault of the people, rather than looking at organizational structures, systems and ways of doing things (organizational culture) as the root of performance problems. When we perceive that the problem is with the indi vidual, we develop solutions that address individual problems. But what if the problem, or a large part, is with the organizational culture? What if an organi zational culture that prides itself on hard work, on 50 to 60 hour work weeks goes overboard? Could performance problems not be the result of uncommitted, slackers, but from overcommitted doers who are afraid to say no because the culture punishes those who do so.

"Fixing" individuals when the problem stems from the system only ensures that there always will be people to "fix." If your organizational surveys (if you do them at all) tell you that certain groups of people (women, people of color, older persons, for example) are less likely to get hired or promoted than other groups, then a certain bell should ring...one that wakes us up to problems in the system. If certain groups of employees have consistently higher turnover rates compared to others, then we should recognize that there might me an underlying problem with the way those groups are being treated, or at least in how they perceive they are being treated. In general, a high turnover rate in one group suggests that there potentially is a "system problem," not necessarily a "people problem."

Poor employee performance results from a number of things including stress, not feeling included or valued, hopelessness and lack of opportunity. But if we rarely consider that organizational culture could be inducing negative stress on certain groups of people, then we often see under performing employees, not people who could thrive in the right environment.

Some people in our organizations are seen as "problem people," and we deal with them from that perspective. But our approach to people issues might change a little, maybe a lot, if we recognize that people issues could be the result of sys temic or organizational flaws.

This perspective, however, often is hard for people in managerial or leader ship positions to accept. The rationalization being, "If I can make it, why can't they?" Rarely is thought given to the disproportionate amount of barriers that im pede some people, and not others. Why? Because we all know that the "playing field is level," just like we know that everything we read and see on television is true.

Does your "system" or organizational culture include everyone? Or does it subtly say, "If you look and act a certain way, then you'll do fine here." If it's the latter, and you want to be able to attract and retain the best and brightest in a more diverse world, then changes must occur. The first step might be accepting that systems and culture issues may be at the root of more observable "people issues," and that "fixing" people could be a waste of time, energy and money. If we can take that first step, we might recognize that the major reason behind the "fixing people" approach is that it's easier to fix people (that is, get rid of them) than to fix systems. The latter is a long, slow and often painful process, but one that, if done right, produces sustainable, lasting benefits.

A number of innocent, hard working bees lost their lives before I covered the tube that allowed them into our house. For some reason, I saw the bees as the problem. Once I figured out that the system needed fixing, I was able to come up with a permanent solution that's better both for the bees and my family. Now, my oldest son no longer nags me about killing innocent bees. And come next spring, my wife's garden will be even more beautiful because there will be more bees to pollinate her flowers. Father of the Year may be lost, but now I'm in the running for Husband of the Year!

Diversity has sometimes about counting people.
Inclusion is always about making people count.
~ Steve L. Robbins ~

30
"Bizeer" Gummies

"SO guys, what would you like for a snack before bed time?" I asked as my three sons and I drove home one night. Nicholas and Zachary, the two oldest, quickly responded in unison, "Fruit roll-ups, Dad!" "

"Now there's good eating," I thought. And getting people to eat sticky, fruit-flavored paper is just plain marketing genius. I looked back at Jacob, our 2-year old, who hadn't put in his order. He seemed to be processing an algorithm in deciding what he wanted. "What would you like, Jacob?"

"Umm, umm, umm...bizeer gummies."

"What kind of gummies?" I asked for clarification.

"Bizeer gummies!" he said confidently.

I searched my brain for a toddler to adult language translation program. Nothing. What in the heck are bizeer gummies? Maybe I was losing my hearing. Should have listened when my mom warned me about going to Bee Gees and Andy Gibb concerts. (And they said Disco was harmless entertainment.)

"Can you say that again, Jacob? What would you like for a snack?"

"Bizeer gummies!" he said again, this time with a look and tone that made me feel like I was the language challenged person in this dialogue. "I want bizeer gummies."

A Ph.D. in communication and still I floundered. What could this little 2-year-old alien be talking about? I had encountered little alien forms of communication in the past with my other sons, but this was a different dialect. "Gummies," I understood. But this "bizeer" word did not register.

"Say it one more time, Jacob. What would you like for a snack?"

I turned my head to see smoke coming from the top of Jacob's head. He looked at me with eyebrows scowled and fired another round of verbal bullets, "I WANT BIZEER GUMMIES!"

Still nothing. I had a sense of what the Axis powers must have been feeling during World War II as they tried to crack the code of the Navajo language. Now, I was frustrated. Not as frustrated as my son, but still frustrated.

Just as I was about to throw in the translation towel, a voice spoke up from the back of our minivan, "I know what Jacob wants." These words should have brought joy to my heart, but a mild anger gripped me instead. Speaking with calmness that belied my true feelings, I asked Nicholas, my eldest son, why he didn't say something sooner. All I got back was, "I don't know."

He's not even a teenager and already he doesn't know things. "So what does Jacob want, Nicholas?" I asked, eagerly awaiting some complex explanation to decipher the toddler talk.

"He wants Buzz Light Year gummies," my son responded non-chalantly, as if to suggest that I received my Ph.D. by mail order.

"Of course, Buzz Light Year gummies," I said to myself. It makes perfect sense. Say "Buzz Light Year" fast enough, with a slurring of the words, and you get "bizeer." My epiphany came just as we pulled into our driveway.

When I got in the house I asked my wife if she knew what "bizeer gummies" were, just to reassure myself that other adults also are ignorant about toddler talk. "Of course!" she said with that "how-did-men-come-to-run-the-world?" look on her face. "Bizeer gummies are Buzz Light Year gummies. You would have known that if you did more grocery shopping with your sons."

"Ouch! Ouch! and Ouch!" Just twist the knife now that it's inserted. In a span of 10 minutes my youngest son taught me how frustrating it can be when one is not well understood, and my dear, loving wife underscored the fact that to understand others, you must get to know them. And to get to know them, you must take intentional steps to spend time with them.

We've all heard the statement that you can't understand that which you do not know. But how many of us actually take to heart the fundamental lesson in that statement? To get to know people, you have to interact with them. And by inter act, I do not mean polite, yet insincere "drive-by hello's" while passing through the hall. Those don't count. Real, substantive interaction means taking time to hang out, to communicate and learn about one another.

Fundamentally, communication is the process of creating shared meaning and understanding. Even in this age of proliferating electronic communication, there still is no substitute for face to face contact when developing relationships. The more time we spend with others, the more we tend to learn about them. The more we learn about them, the greater chance that there will be fewer misun derstandings. Strangers, once distant, become less strange. So, investing time in communicating with others is like taking out an insurance policy against lack of understanding in the future.

While it is relatively easy to set aside time for people we already know, it's much harder when it comes to people we don't know. If the United States is be coming more racially and culturally diverse, then it is imperative for individuals and organizations that want to be culturally competent to take out that "insurance policy." That means investing time in getting to know people we see as different from ourselves. The more time invested, the greater chance we will learn that we have a lot in common, or that any substantive differences are launching pads for greater learning.

When we don't take the time to create shared meaning and understanding, we assure ourselves of future communication problems. Misunderstanding and lack of understanding often result in frustration and anger for all parties. It doesn't take a rocket scientist, or even a Ph.D. in communication, to know that frustrated and angry people generally are not beneficial to organizations.

It's in the best interest of organizations to encourage an investment in re lationship building among their personnel, on and off the clock. And not just building relationships between people who feel comfortable with each other, but with people who do not right away find a lot in common. It is the latter situation with which we all will more frequently rub shoulders in the future, and in which the potential for lack of understanding and misunderstanding will be high.

This lack of understanding of others often occurs when there is "noise" in the message transfer. By noise, I mean anything that hinders the receiver from get ting the message as the sender intended. Noise can be anything from a different language to distracting non-verbal signs to having lenses and filters that distort the message. Noise is not necessarily anyone's fault. But we must recognize it as a cause of communication problems, and it must be overcome for effective communication to occur.

A combination of factors contributed to the "noise" between my son Jacob and me. One factor was my lack of the correct filter to decipher the word "bi zeer." Another was my son's way of pronouncing words that did not fit my own method and style of oral communication. It was unfamiliar. The former is easier to fix than the latter. All I needed to do was spend more time with my son to familiarize myself with the way he talked. If I would have spent more time with him, I'd have heard him say "bizeer" when holding onto a package of Buzz Light Year gummies. The connection would have been obvious. The latter is an issue of child speech development that most likely will be overcome with time. Neither Jacob nor myself can do much to muffle this type of "noise."

So I am left really with only one course of action if I want to fix the noise problem immediately. I need to spend more time with Jacob, to get to know him and his method of communication better. It's really just that simple to overcome "understanding" problems with others who may communicate or act a little dif ferently than you do. Yep, that's right, we need to allocate more time for getting to know "others." By doing so, we then will foster an environment where creat ing shared meaning is much more possible, where understanding is much more likely and where beneficial relationships are built.

So take out that insurance policy and get to know others with whom you rarely spend time. But remember, insurance policies are obtained over time with regular payments. In the same way, relationships are built over time, with regular and frequent payments of attention. It's hard work that often yields lasting ben efits.

People generally only see what they look for and
only hear what they listen for.
~ Harper Lee ~

31
A Difference in Weight

IT'S a new year and like a pre programmed goose I've made my annual re turn to our local health club. You know, to shed a few pounds and transform my average Hyundai body into a stunning BMW physique. No, really, I will.

My first trip back was invigorating, so to speak. There's nothing like the smell of a men's locker room to shock one out of the exercise doldrums. The aroma of sweaty towels spiced with athletic club brand underarm spray brought back faint memories of my collegiate athletic days. Throw in a pinch of Ben Gay and the recollection would have been complete. Someone should bottle that smell and put it into one of those "first contact" capsules that are sent into outer space. It would be an effective pre emptive strike against alien invasion.

After leaving the locker room, I made my way to the stationary bikes for some cardio time. As I stood there looking at the rows of bikes and bike like machines, I marveled at human rationality. It takes a special kind of species to develop contraptions that require significant physical fuel, but in the end takes the rider nowhere. At least these things don't add too much to the global warming prob lem.

As I eased myself into one of these bike machines I was prompted to input some information. Manual or automatic? Workout level? Oh, the days when one would just hop on a bike and start peddling...and actually go somewhere. Yes,

I know I could still do that, but you try to ride a bike in the snowy landscape of a Michigan January. Plus, it's so gauche to travel real miles in the 21st century when one can navigate virtual miles.

I was feeling good about myself as I approached my goal of thirty minutes on the bike...29:57, 29:58, 29:59, 30:00!!! Done. As I stopped pedaling, I pressed the "Summary" button on the bike to reassure myself that there was a reason for the sweat flowing from my body and the pain pulsing through my legs. I really didn't care how many virtual miles I had pedaled, I wanted to know how many real calories I had burned. And there it was on the screen before me. I had "rid den" 4.7 electronic miles and shed an amazing 150 calories. Wow! In the short span of thirty minutes I rid myself of the 12 ounce can of Coke that I had guz zled in thirty seconds at lunch. The reality of that input output equation, though depressing, would not deter me from my fitness goals. I went off to the place where serious body sculptors go...the free weights. Yes, for all of you exercise neophytes, free weights are it! At least, that's what I've been told. And I wanted to be in with it!

My it time was initiated with some bench presses to re build my atrophying chest. Big, defined chests on men are the equivalent of the colorful plumes of a male peacock, the mane on a lion or the horns on a bull. Indeed, a maximized pectoralis maximus, or "pecs" in body building lingo, separates men from boys. That's what Lou Ferrigno once said, and who am I to argue with the Incredible Hulk?

I started off with 45 pound plates, and when you add the 45 pound bar it to taled 135 pounds. Not bad for a little, 35 plus something guy like me. Though it was difficult, I was able to do ten repetitions with some strength to spare.

Feeling the testosterone welling inside, I put on additional ten pound plates, for a total of 155 pounds. Again, it was difficult, especially the last three, but I pressed another ten reps. Surely, I could do no more. I found some 5 pound plates and was now up to 165 pounds.

I rested a little before attacking my third set. Okay, maybe more than a little. You have to understand that in the gym, time is different. It's like human and dog years. A minute of gym time is actually seven real minutes, so in gym time, I really only rested 45 seconds.

Grabbing the bar for my third set, I pushed with all my might to lift it off the rests. Breathe in, push up, down easy, air out..."one." Breathe in, push up, down easy, air out..."two." Breathe in, push up, down easy, air out..."three." And on to "ten." I did it! The last four or five reps were extremely tough. (In lifting terms, tough is determined by the facial contortions and guttural sounds one makes.) Finished with that set, I sat up to see if anyone was watching. Like many males in the gym, I want others to notice my muscle-flexing accomplish ments. Sadly, the few others who were there either had not seen or were too busy searching out their own audiences.

As I began taking the weights off the bar, the chest pounding maleness in me kicked in one more time. I figured I could do more, even though I hadn't lifted more than 165 pounds in years. Surely, I could do 175. It's just ten more pounds. I found five-pound plates, and as I put on those little plates I thought about get ting a spotter, someone who would be there just in case I was unable to lift the weight off my chest. Nah, I had just done ten reps at 165 pounds, and 175 is just a fraction more. How tough could that be?

Lying on the bench once again, I placed my hands on the bar, closed my eyes and envisioned lifting a feather. I told myself it was only ten more pounds. After thirty gym seconds, I was mentally ready. I sucked a mountain of air into my diaphragm for support and gave a big push to get the bar off its launch pad. With 175 pounds above my chest, held up by two locked arms, I thought about the task at hand. Either I successfully lift the weight or I crush my chest. I couldn't turn back. I had to forge ahead. And so I did.

I let the bar down slowly until it nearly reached my chest and then gave a tremendous push. The bar went up a few inches and stalled. "Uh oh!" I thought. "You're a volcano!" I told myself. "Erupt." I strained to get the bar higher, but couldn't. I felt my arms weaken further. The Dylithium crystals were running out of energy. Just as my arms were about to buckle, a guy nearby came over and asked if I needed help. "How observant," I thought. "Yes, yes," I stammered as the thought of concave pectorals flashed through my mind.

After getting the bar back on the rests, I thanked the man for his help. As he turned to walk away, he suggested that I get a spotter next time. Indeed, having a spotter would be a good idea. I looked around to see if anyone had seen this embarrassing debacle. As luck would have it, this time I had an audience.

So I bet you're asking what this story has to do with diversity and inclusion. This "teachable moment" is not necessarily about those issues, but about sen sitivity to the backgrounds and experiences of others, about understanding that another's life journey affects how they interpret the "weight" of events.

Every now and then an incident happens in the workplace that appears very "light" and innocuous to some, but is significantly "heavy" and disturbing to oth ers. You know what I'm talking about. It's the "innocent, I didn't mean anything by it" gay joke told in the lunchroom. It's having a brand new refrigerator in the air-conditioned main office area where mostly "degreed" folks work and an older refrigerator on the hot, assembly line where many high school grads work. It's having calendars of scantily clad women on walls and locker room doors. In the big scheme of things, and taken as singular, disconnected events, these types of things might be seen as light and trivial.

If you are the one who makes the gay joke, the person in the main office or the man with the calendar, you perceive your actions as "innocent" and "impo tent." In fact, if an offended party were to bring up the offense, you and others with the same mental framework would tell "those people" to lighten up, to quit being so sensitive. It is unlikely that you would think about why it could be "so offensive." It is unlikely that you would think of these "isolated" incidents as links in a long chain of connected events. You will see "light" when others will see "heavy."

Well, let's take a look at my trip to the gym to see how the weight of an event can be differently interpreted. So-called "out-group" people, such as minorities, homosexuals, the homeless and those in poverty, carry the continuous weight of discrimination and exclusion in U.S. society. Years of being left on the fringe of society are like the thirty minute bike ride. It tires you out. Often, you exert lots of energy trying to make your way up the societal and workplace ladder, but you make little progress because of built in, systemic barriers. But you don't give up.

While still tired, you then have to endure, sometimes on a daily basis, the reality that you don't have access to the same doors others easily walk through. Maybe it's your age. Maybe it's the color of your skin or your socio economic status. Maybe it's your gender or sexual orientation. Whatever your out group marker is, society has turned the things that identify you into 45 pound weights that limit what you can pursue and achieve. But you don't give up. You press on trying to make the in group recognize the reality of the additional weights you are holding up. Very few of them hear and see how "tough" it is. They let you know through various overt and subtle means that your pain is imaginary, or blown out of proportion. This process of persuading others that the barriers in your path are real serve as the ten pound plates that continue to zap your energy. Your muscles are now burning, but you don't give up.

Next, you are slapped in the face when others whom you thought "got it" don't carry through on the commitment they so passionately made to "do some thing." You find out that their passion only exists in attitude, not behavior. They blow over when a strong wind comes along. They tell you to not make a big fuss, because they don't want to ruffle the organizational feathers, to create a hostile environment for the majority. It's really hard now with an additional five pounds on either side, but you raise your emotional bar to survive the letdown. You don't give up.

Finally, under the heavy stress of being invisible, unheard and marginalized, the "playful" jokes about women's work or the "innocent" references to "those lazy people" are like the 2½-pound weights. A little bit of additional weight can make an already heavy bar unbearable. You have no more energy to lift the bar, let alone hold it up. The bar comes crashing down and everybody sees. But they don't see the cumulative weight and burden. They only see the last little weights that you tried to lift. And because they are unable or unwilling to see the whole truth, they can't and won't serve as the much needed spotter that all of us need when things get rough.

The weight of an environment that is not as inclusive as it can be is extremely heavy if you are unfortunate enough to be in the out group. In this type of en vironment, it only takes a little incident to make the proverbial mountain out of a molehill. And when this occurs, the whole organization suffers. Some suffer because they are hit with lawsuits. Just ask Coca Cola, Texaco and Denny's. Others suffer because they have to take time away from core activities to deal with issues that could have been solved with proactive measures or if more people had taken on the responsibility of being attentive spotters.

Do you have what it takes to be a spotter? Are you sensitive enough to others' viewpoints and experiences to understand how a molehill becomes a mountain? And are you strong enough to argue for the mountain when the majority of people around you only see a molehill? If the answer is no, you may want to make some new personal goals on this front. If you achieve your goals, I think you'll be pleasantly surprised at the image you see the next time you look in the mirror.

And you won't even have to smell a locker room in the process.

Comfort is the mortal enemy of creativity.
~ Steve L. Robbins ~

32
Lion Chase

"LET'S play lion chase." That's the greeting my three sons gave me the other night as I entered our house after a long day of work. It wasn't "Hi dad, we love you, glad you're home" or "Hi dad, you're the greatest, how was your day?" It wasn't even a simple "Hi dad." It was perfectly clear that at this particular mo ment they were missing a piece from their play puzzle, and that piece had just walked through the door.

But I didn't want to play lion chase, which, as it has come to be known in the Robbins household, is a tiring game. It began with our first son, Nicholas, as soon as he started gaining some upright mobility. I would chase him around the house on my hands and knees, and yes, you got it, did my best imitation of a lion. It wasn't a very good imitation, but it didn't have to be because it's really not that difficult to trick a 1-year-old. When this game started, I was a bit younger with a little more energy, a little more time and better knees. Now, well, let's just say I'm a little more "mature."

Like many "mature" people, I often am tired after a day of work. I just want to relax when I get home. You know, kick back on our comfy, purple couch and read the newspaper to learn about all the bad things going on in our world. Is this too much to ask? Apparently, as far as my sons were concerned that day, the answer is "yes."

Though it's an exercise in futility, I tried to get out of playing lion chase, reeling off a number of rational excuses for why I couldn't play and hoping they would understand. They didn't. They are not rational beings.

"I'm tired guys, maybe later" was my first feeble attempt to resist. This never works. I don't even know why I bother. Guess it's the cognitive script I have in responding to my sons' requests. But I hope.

Nicholas, my 7-year-old, looks at me, smiles and fires back, "Yea right, Dad." Where is this "respect for elders" thing that Vietnamese kids are supposed to have? Who's teaching this kid anyway?

My son Zachary, just five years old, then chimes in, "C'mon dad, we want to play lion chase." Timed with the words is a well-packaged leg hug and fake smile that breaks down my defenses. I feel my shields weakening, but they hold up. He's a smart little bugger with an emotional intelligence of someone greater in years...and he knows how to use it. But I know his attack plan, and I divert power to the front shields.

At this point the youngest son, Jacob, waits patiently on the left flank, behind a door, looking for an opening to join the first wave of attack. Zachary looks back at Jacob and seamlessly moves his hug from my left leg to my right. That is Jacob's signal to move forward. With reckless abandon Jacob surges ahead, his radar locked in on my left leg. He sounds the battle cry, "D-A-D-D-Y." The impact of the hit rocks me back on my heels. The shields are now down to 40 percent, weakening to dangerous levels.

Instinctively, Nicholas senses my impending peril. He knows the end is near, and fires from all PHASER banks. "If you play lion chase, we'll clean our rooms." My shields drain further...30 percent, 20 percent. Zachary and Jacob squeeze my legs even harder...10 percent. As I am about to surrender, the most powerful force in this sector of the universe descends on the battle zone. MOM has arrived.

My wife enters the conflict with PHASERS set on stun. She hails us on all frequencies. Calmly, but powerfully, she gives both warring parties an uncondi tional directive. "Shhhhh, you're too loud, Natalie is sleeping." My sons quickly quiet down. They know the voice of an omnipotent being when they hear it. "Natalie hasn't taken a nap all day. If you wake her up, you'll have to go to your rooms for some quiet time." My sons voluntarily power down their PHASERS. I lower what's left of my shields. A tension-filled stillness overcomes the room.

Satisfied that her message has been communicated, MOM leaves the room. But knowing her sons well, she quickly returns with three simple, but forceful words that all primitive beings understand, "I mean it." She reinforces the words with a stare and nod of her head that confirms the finality of the battle. My sons and I recognize that MOM is not in the best of moods. A clingy 8 month old with an aversion to napping, in a house filled with three mini-male power packs, can sour even the most loving and omnipotent of all loving and omnipotent be ings. History has taught all the males in the family that it's best not to mess with MOM during these times.

But, one of the boys is suddenly hit with historic amnesia. Somewhere in Jacob's still developing 3 year old brain, the connection between actions and consequences has not been fused. As Nicholas, Zachary and I begin to leave the room, Jacob powers up his weapons and again locks in on my left leg while firing his thrusters, "Let's play lion chase."

"This is not good, not good at all," I thought. You see, being the third son, Jacob has had to find ways to attract attention. So over the course of time he has learned to be loud. In fact, Jacob has developed two settings when it comes to oral communication, loud and louder. And he has no mute button. His zesty outburst spells doom for the rest of us. Theoretically, there is nothing faster than the speed of light, but MOM's return to the room challenged that notion. "I told you what would happen. Down to your rooms, boys."

Nicholas and Zachary protest, pleading their innocence. "We didn't do any thing. It was Jacob. He's the one being loud." Oh, the strength of brotherly bonds when consequences are on the line. "It's not fair, we didn't..."

Recognizing the futility in Nicholas and Zachary's attempts to influence MOM, I interrupt mid-sentence, "Go to your rooms, guys. Now's not the time." If you think I intervened to shield my sons from further consequences, you have it all wrong. I did it purely for self preservation. I might be a few PHASERS short of fully loaded, but I am smart enough to know that I suffer when my wife is not in a good mood. It doesn't matter who is the cause. When MOM is not at her best, we are in a "No" environment. No joy, no fun, no communication and no you know what.

As I walked my sons down to their rooms, I felt a little bad that I just didn't play lion chase with them when they first asked. In a very Clintonian way, I felt their pain. To ease my guilt, I told them I would play lion chase with them after Natalie woke from her nap...and after they cleaned their rooms. With that offer, smiles reappeared on their faces and they raced to their rooms with warp speed to begin cleaning.

If you are part of diversity and inclusion initiatives in your organization, you know that resistance to those programs are inevitable. There are people like yourself (like my sons trying to make me play "lion chase") who are pushing and pulling others to join the organization's inclusion efforts. And there are al ways people who resist your efforts. Yes, they are the ones who don't want to play "lion chase." You try to get their buy-in and commitment, but they refuse to listen. Or, if they do listen, they do not hear. They have feeble excuses built on poor, outdated information. They often aren't willing even to open their minds to the possibility that a more inclusive organization offers benefits to everyone.

The battle between those who want to "play lion chase" and those who don't makes the organization vulnerable in many areas. Often, this battle takes place at middle and lower levels of organizations. It is at this time that the leadership of the organization or some other "powerful force" needs to communicate clearly the benefits of action and the consequences of inaction, just as my wife made clear to us "boys" the consequences of not complying with her directive. All parties involved suffer. Maybe it's just some people who suffer in the short term, but it's all of us in the long term.

Organizations that aren't making progress with their diversity and inclusion initiatives will, in a more diverse future, find themselves with PHASERS while their competition will be armed with more powerful photon torpedoes. More prepared competitors who have embraced diversity and inclusion will be better able to attract and retain the best and brightest. As such, they'll be in a better position to "attack" vexing problems because of the diversity of perspectives and cumulative cognitive power they possess. Not only will these better armed organizations be able to attack their problems (and markets) more effectively, they'll also be in a better position to defend themselves when the outside envi ronment turns hostile. These organizations are more likely to hold their position when the economy sours. When other organizations are losing market share be cause they don't take serious the bottom line impact of changing demographics, these better-armed organizations will find creative ways to take advantage of the changes.

For example, they will be better able to capitalize on a people of color market that represents nearly two trillion dollars worth of collective buying power. Or on a gay and lesbian population that is increasingly an affluent, better educated and more powerful consumer force; Or on an aging population that is a gold mine of wisdom, stability and, yes, buying power.

Better "armed" organizations are less likely to be fending off discrimination lawsuits and less likely to have high employee turnover rates, both of which negatively and significantly impact an organization's efficiency and bottom line. When other organizations are laying off, the better armed organizations are maintaining, even hiring.

So the message is clear. Everyone, the entire organization, benefits when the organization is diverse and inclusive. Alternatively, everyone will suffer when the organization is homogeneous and exclusive. While the message is clear, sometimes it requires the intervention of a powerful force (like leadership) to get it through the thick skulls of those who don't want to "play lion chase." Some times your organization needs a "MOM" to descend on the battlefield to get the message through. Does your organization have a "MOM" that effectively can communicate the consequences of inaction with respect to diversity and inclu sion? If you don't, you better get one.

Every organization needs a MOM.

Preconceived notions are the locks on the door to wisdom.
~ Merry Browne ~

33
Inaccurate Maps

"WHERE could this place be?" I said to myself as I drove down the street in my little rental car, searching for my hotel. According to the map and directions I was given, my final destination was somewhere on Grand Street. But Grand Street was nowhere to be found. At least, not by me. Now if I had been look ing for Jackson Street, Washington Street, Jefferson Street or some other street named after U.S. presidents, I would have been just fine. But I was not fine. I was becoming frustrated as each passing street reminded me of my high school history class. The instructions in my hand said nothing about all these streets. All I was given was the basics, "Get off the highway, turn right on Central Avenue, drive a few miles, then right on Grand Street, the hotel is on the right." As I drove further and further I became more and more frustrated. I was consoled, however, by the thought that if I ever wanted a street named after me, I could earn big points by becoming President of the United States.

With my anxiety level quickly rising like a backed up toilet, thoughts of stop ping to ask for directions entered my mind. Of course, they quickly drowned in a flood of testosterone. After all, I am male, and there are certain male stereotypes that I am called to live up to mindlessly. So powerful are these stereotypes that I too have fallen prey to their beckoning. To a man, stopping for directional assis tance is tantamount to raising the white flag of defeat. This I could not do. Such an act is treason in the court of maleness.

Treason or not, I'm quite sure the person driving behind me gladly would have raised the flag for me, and waved it with great vigor. While I understand that getting caught behind a person driving 20 miles per hour in a 40 mile per hour zone is excruciatingly painful, there was nothing I could do. Well, okay, there was nothing else I was willing to do.

After driving another 10 minutes or so with no Grand Street in sight, I pulled over to the side of the road to get my bearings. Understand that I was not stopping to ask for help. I was just stopping to get a more complete look at the map and directions I was given. There is a big difference between stopping and stopping to ask for directions, a distinction made clear in the SMRB (Secret Male Rules Book). A few privileged men are awarded this coveted book of life upon completion of male training camp. Graduates of this camp are a principled and rules driven group of people. That's what one half of the population says. The other half claims that males are just stubborn creatures comprised mainly of a self absorbing ego.

Sitting in my decidedly Spartan rental car with other vehicles whizzing by like they knew where they were going, I examined the map and directions more closely. For some reason, I was so anxious and nervous that I actually was shaking. I needed more information, more details to soothe my uncertainty. Studying the map to get a better orientation and understanding of this new and unfamiliar environment, I looked to see if I had missed anything, a landmark, a street or other detail. But I couldn't find any additional information that could assist me. I thought perhaps there was a second page to the fax that was missing, but the faxed page in my hand read "1 of 1" at the top. That was all I was sent. There was no more.

Now what was I going to do? The situation wasn't amusing any more. I don't even think it was amusing to start with. It was late and I didn't know where I was or what I was going to do next. At these times in my life I have learned to stop, take a breather, and offer up a succinct, but powerful prayer. Though the words are slightly different each time, the message is basically the same, "I don't know where I am going, God. I need your help."

And so with my prayer offered up, I turned back onto Central Avenue, driving with a little less anxiety but still lost. Within 30 seconds, my prayer was answered. To my left was a big billboard advertising some type of restaurant   I can't recall which one   and at the bottom of the billboard was the response to my request, "Right on Grand Street, 3 Miles Ahead."

"Yippee," I blurted out loud, just like my 3-year-old son does when his prayer for a chocolate covered donut with sprinkles is answered in the affirmative. I would be in a nice hotel room soon.

Sitting safely in my room, I reflected on where I had been just 20 minutes earlier. It hit me that the root cause of much of my anxiety could be traced back to the fact that I did not have a very good map of where I was going. The map and directions I had been given lacked the details that would have helped me navigate my way through an unfamiliar city. Though I wanted to blame the person who had provided the map, I knew my sails should be raised to catch the winds of guilt. I could have, in fact, should have looked at the map more closely before leaving the airport. In doing so, I probably would have noticed that the directions and details were too simple, especially for such a big city.

It has been written that we live in a world of "territories" and "maps." Territories can be thought of as the actual physical place that exists in our 3 dimensional world. Maps can be understood as the 2 dimensional representations of those territories. As many of us know, maps vary in accuracy. The more accurate a map is, the easier it is for the map's user to find a particular location. The map I received lacked some details that would have been helpful.

Like bad "maps" of physical "territories," we often have bad or incomplete information when it comes to real people. If our people maps are bad enough, when we actually encounter the "real thing" there is a tendency to become anxious, uncertain, disoriented and even fearful. And in those states, we are more likely to react negatively than positively. We are more likely to be exclusive than inclusive. We are more likely to submit to our stereotypical maps than to embrace the reality of the "territory." In other words, if we are programmed with incomplete maps, like we all generally are when it comes to people different than ourselves, and we make no attempts to create more accurate maps, then we should not be surprised to find ourselves frustrated and fearful during encounters with other people and the reality of their "territories."

As our world becomes increasingly diverse, we all would do well to create and develop more accurate people maps. To create better maps means to expose ourselves to as many different people "territories" as possible. There is no short cut. No book you can read, no play you can attend, no PBS show you can watch that will take the place of direct interaction with people different than ourselves. While books, plays and television programs certainly can help, they are easy substitutes that we often use to rationalize our less than pioneering spirit. Any substitute, by definition, is just another map that lacks the critical details.

In the process of acquiring better maps, we likely will find ourselves in better position to embrace the diversity that exists around us. With better maps, we will be more likely to see that differences in others are not necessarily better or worse, just different. We likely will discover a vein of gold instead of chunks of coal. Maybe then we will look around to discover that we don't even need any more maps because we know the territories so well.

Closing Thought

IN his first full year on the PGA Tour, Tiger Woods went to Augusta, Georgia and shot a record 18 under par to win the Masters golf tournament by an amazing 12 strokes. Yes, his closest competitor, the second place person shot 6 under par. In many other years that 6-under score would have topped the field. Tiger ended up winning three more tournaments that year and climbed to a No. 1 world ranking in his 42nd week as a pro. Voted the Associated Press Male Athlete of the year in 1997, his short stint on the PGA tour had already netted him six titles, a lifetime achievement for most PGA Tour players.

He was hailed by the media as the next golf superstar capable of breaking the achievements of Arnold Palmer and Jack Nicklaus – combined! His amateur record had already told everyone he was going to be good, if not great, but to surpass Jack and Arnie? There were more believers following Tiger's magical first year.

His second year did not produce the same fireworks as the first. Though he ended the year as the No. 1 ranked golfer with 19 out of 20 cuts made, he only won one tournament, and it was not one of the four majors (i.e., Masters, U.S. Open, British Open, PGA Championship). As Tiger will tell you, his primary goal is to win majors. Everything else he does is done with winning majors in mind. Talk about Tiger being as good as Jack and Arnie diminished.

When initially asked why he wasn't winning as many tournaments as many expected him to win, he doesn't offer much, only to remind the media that he was still the top ranked golfer and had made 19 cuts – pointing to the positives as I'm sure his sports psychologist told him to do. Throughout the 1998 season many speculated as to why Tiger wasn't winning. As the golf world came to find out, Tiger was changing his swing. Yes, the same swing that had already netted him three straight major amateur titles and six professional titles including the Masters by the age of 22. Many thought he was crazy for changing his swing, especially during a successful run. They could understand changing a swing in the midst of a slump, but not while one is tearing up the field. When asked why the swing change, Tiger simply says, "I want to be better." He basically told them that his body is changing, golf courses were changing, the players around him were changing, equipment was changing and all the change required changes from him. He understood that a changing golf world required changes in him if he was to compete at the highest levels. Still, many questioned his swing change, suggesting that Tiger was getting bad advice.

Tiger silenced his critiques in 1999 winning eight tour events including his second major, the PGA Championship. He finished the year with four consecu tive victories. Asked about the big turnaround from the previous year, he smiled and told the media that the work he put into changing his swing paid off, as he expected it would. He would later recall a story in which, during a practice ses sion, he called his then coach, Butch Harmon, and said, "I got it." He said it was that day that he felt fully confident in his swing, confident enough to trust it dur ing all four rounds of a golf tournament. He had been working on the swing for 18 months.

The new swing served him immensely in a once in a lifetime fourth season as he won three consecutive majors, and a total of nine tournaments. He collected his fourth consecutive major in 2001, completing what people ended up calling the "Tiger Slam" (winning four straight majors, but not in a calendar year). The next two years brought more titles and more majors. But in 2003, though he won five tournaments, none was a major, and then the unthinkable happened in 2004, he relinquished his position as the No. 1 player in the world to Vijay Singh – a spot Tiger had held for 264 consecutive weeks.

2003 and 2004 passed without a major victory. Many speculated about the reasons for Tiger's demise. Was it because he got married and there were other distractions? Was it because the other players on tour had caught up? Had Tiger lost his edge because he had no true rival to push him? Many thought it was be cause he was changing his swing, again.

Whenever there was talk about his swing change, many questioned why he was changing it again. Tiger echoed what he said the last time this happened, "I want to get better." In some interviews he would give the Tiger smile, his big teeth shining in the camera lights, basically saying to people, "Just wait and see." Again, he recognized the world was changing around him and he needed to once again change.

The world didn't have to wait long to hear Tiger's roar. Tiger won a mess of tournaments in 2005 and 2006 including four more majors. His spectacular 2006 season was accomplished in the wake of his father's death. His swing changes and other adjustments paid off again. Guess what he might do in 2007 or 2008? Does "swing change" come to mind?

Tiger is a great example of someone who is mindful of the dynamic world he lives and plays in – a world constantly changing, ever in motion, variables always varying. In his mind to be the best, he had to make changes, and in mak ing those changes he was willing to take a step back so he could eventually take three or four steps forward. He was willing to sacrifice a few short-term goals to achieve his main goal, his main priority—topping Jack Nicklaus' record of 18 major victories. Tiger already has 12 majors notched in his bag and he's only 31 years old. In golf, many say players do not reach their peak until their mid thirties. I feel sorry for the other golfers on the PGA tour.

What can we all learn from Tiger and his approach to achieving success in a changing world, when the variables are constantly in motion? I work in some environments where the motto is "150 years of tradition unimpeded by progress." My guess is that if Tiger took this approach, he would still be a very good golfer, but he would be no where near where he is today in making his claim of being the best golfer of all time. Tiger is never satisfied with the status quo, never content with what is, always mindful of what could be and the need to "get better." We could learn much from Tiger's mindful, committed and purposeful approach to golf. Are you and your organization willing to learn?

If so, as the ad campaign in which Tiger is prominent says, "Go ahead, be a Tiger!" Roar a loud roar. You are on a journey of great work that requires a mindfulness to changes in our world, and a willingness and commitment to meet the demands of those changes.

I selfishly would like to hear your roar because I'm on a mission to get more allies in this work. The more of you there are with me, the more we make this a better place for everyone. Remember, whether we call this work diversity, diversity and inclusion, cultural competency or whatever seems in style at the time, the bottom line for why we should all do this is because people matter, and caring about people matters. The power of caring will surface in higher employee engagement, higher patent satisfaction scores, reaching more consumers, leaving no children behind, and so much more! When we genuinely care about others we unleash the power of inclusion, and in doing so we will create a world where more people are able to pursue life, liberty and happiness.

Printed in the United States
90230LV00002B/172-264/A